Harvey Special Reports Series

Discrimination: the New Law

agth

Harvey Special Reports Series
Discrimination: the New Law

A guide to the new Regulations on
race, religion or belief, sexual orientation and disability

by

Michael Rubenstein

Editor, Industrial Relations Law Reports

Members of the LexisNexis Group worldwide

United Kingdom	LexisNexis UK, a Division of Reed Elsevier (UK) Ltd, Halsbury House, 35 Chancery Lane, LONDON, WC2A 1EL, and 4 Hill Street, EDINBURGH EH2 3JZ
Argentina	LexisNexis Argentina, BUENOS AIRES
Australia	LexisNexis Butterworths, CHATSWOOD, New South Wales
Austria	LexisNexis Verlag ARD Orac GmbH & Co KG, VIENNA
Canada	LexisNexis Butterworths, MARKHAM, Ontario
Chile	LexisNexis Chile Ltda, SANTIAGO DE CHILE
Czech Republic	Nakladatelství Orac sro, PRAGUE
France	Editions du Juris-Classeur SA, PARIS
Germany	LexisNexis Deutschland GmbH, FRANKFURT and MUNSTER
Hong Kong	LexisNexis Butterworths, HONG KONG
Hungary	HVG-Orac, BUDAPEST
India	LexisNexis Butterworths, NEW DELHI
Ireland	LexisNexis, DUBLIN
Italy	Giuffrè Editore, MILAN
Malaysia	Malayan Law Journal Sdn Bhd, KUALA LUMPUR
New Zealand	LexisNexis Butterworths, WELLINGTON
Poland	Wydawnictwo Prawnicze LexisNexis, WARSAW
Singapore	LexisNexis Butterworths, SINGAPORE
South Africa	LexisNexis Butterworths, Durban
Switzerland	Stämpfli Verlag AG, BERNE
USA	LexisNexis, DAYTON, Ohio

© Reed Elsevier (UK) Ltd 2004
Published by LexisNexis UK

A CIP Catalogue record for this book is available from the British Library.

ISBN 0 406 97878 6

Printed and bound in Great Britain by William Clowes Limited, Beccles and London

Visit LexisNexis UK at www.lexisnexis.co.uk

Contents

PART 1

Cross-strand issues

Chapter 1

Chapter 2

Contents

PART II

Strand-specific issues

Chapter 7

Chapter 8

Contents

Table of statutes

Table of cases

Introduction

Welcome to the new world of discrimination law! Discrimination law is being transformed by implementation of three EU Directives.

Major changes to the Race Relations Act came into effect on 19 July 2003 as a result of implementation of the EU Race Discrimination Directive 2000/43. On 1 December 2003, the new right not to be discriminated against on grounds of sexual orientation came into force, and the new right not to be discriminated against on grounds of religion or belief came into force the next day, 2 December 2003. This implements the EU Framework Employment Directive 2000/78. In October 2004, important amendments to the Disability Discrimination Act, transposing that strand of the Framework Directive, will take effect. October 2005 will see a strengthening of the Sex Discrimination Act as a result of the revision to the EU Equal Treatment Directive by Directive 2002/73. And then in October 2006, the last part of the Framework Directive, the new right not to be discriminated against on grounds of age, will be implemented.

Regulations have already been approved by Parliament making these changes to the law on race, sexual orientation, religion or belief and disability, and that is the focus of this edition of this book.

In its October 2002 consultative document *Equality and Diversity: The way ahead*, the Government emphasised that its proposals 'are designed to make equality legislation more coherent and easier to use'. Accordingly, the Government promised that it will 'use the same wording, where appropriate, for all the main concepts: direct discrimination, indirect discrimination, harassment and victimisation.' The Regulations as enacted reflect that commitment, though whether they will make equality legislation 'more coherent' is more problematic.

Because of this structure, it makes sense to look first at the key 'cross-strand' concepts that span race, religion or belief, sexual orientation and disability. In the second part of the book, we then focus on the 'strand-specific' issues in the new Regulations.

Although the Regulations do not apply directly to Northern Ireland, parallel legislation has been introduced there.

Problems of implementation

The Government decided to implement the new discrimination Directives by Regulations made under the European Communities Act 1972, s 2 rather than by primary legislation, which has to pass through all the stages of Parliamentary consideration. This has had a number of consequences.

Unlike primary legislation, Regulations made under the European Communities Act 1972 can go no further than is required by the EU legislation that they are intended to implement. Choosing this route, therefore, meant that discrimination outside the sphere of employment and vocational training could not be dealt with by the Regulations. That means that there is no remedy for a gay couple denied a double bed in a hotel or a Muslim abused by a barman in pub. The same is likely to be true of age discrimination outside the employment sphere as the Government is committed to implement these by Regulations also.

In contrast, the protection against discrimination on grounds of race, disability or sex is much more comprehensive, thus suggesting a hierarchy of rights, as discussed below. The narrower scope for the new rights is without doubt anomalous, but Government is also understandably wary about placing too many burdens on business.

What is really indefensible is the incoherence produced in the Race Relations Act by taking this route. This has resulted in two different tests for indirect discrimination in employment, two different legal standards relating to racial harassment at work, two different burdens of proof in employment cases, depending on whether the discrimination is alleged to be on grounds of race, ethnic or national origins on the one hand, or nationality or colour on the other hand. The Government could have avoided this by implementing the Race Discrimination Directive by primary legislation. One can only presume that this was not done because it might have led to political pressure to implement the other strands by primary legislation as well.

Moreover, by choosing to go down the statutory instrument route rather than using a Bill, the Government was unable to make any changes to the Regulations once they had been laid before Parliament. This meant that they were unable to correct any errors or omissions, which placed great pressure on the drafters to get it right first time.

Whether they entirely did so is questionable, in my view. There are a number of areas where arguments can – and doubtless will – be made that the Directives have not been implemented correctly by the Regulations, or that their drafting does not achieve what the Government intended. For example:

- The Religion or Belief Regulations do not expressly provide protection against discrimination on grounds of absence of belief.
- The Sexual Orientation Regulations contain an awkwardly-worded genuine occupational requirement exclusion relating to employment for the purposes of an organised religion that has been challenged by way of judicial review as failing to implement the Framework Employment Directive correctly and contravening the European Convention on Human Rights.
- The Framework Employment Directive provides that an 'instruction to discriminate' shall 'be deemed to be discrimination'. That has not been transposed into either the Religion or Belief or the Sexual Orientation Regulations, presumably because proceedings in respect of an instruction to discriminate on grounds of race, disability or sex can only be brought by the relevant statutory enforcement agency, and no enforcement agency has yet been given jurisdiction to deal with complaints of sexual orientation discrimination or discrimination on grounds of religion or belief.
- The definition of indirect discrimination in the Directives merely refers to a provision, criterion or practice that 'would put' persons at a disadvantage. However, the Regulations add the further requirement that the provision, criterion or practice must be one that actually 'puts' the applicant at the disadvantage.
- The test of justification for indirect discrimination in the Directives requires an employer to show that the provision, criterion or practice is 'objectively justified by a legitimate aim and the means of achieving that aim are appropriate and necessary', whereas the Regulations require the employer to show that it is 'a proportionate means of achieving a legitimate aim.'
- The genuine occupational requirement exceptions fail to replicate the language of the

Directives by specifying that any GOR must have a 'legitimate objective'.

One of the other disadvantages of implementing the new rights on religion or belief and sexual orientation via Regulations under the European Communities Act 1972 is that there is no power conferred on anyone to issue a Code of Practice giving guidance and practical examples. The DTI has partially filled the gap by producing very useful 'explanatory notes' and publishing them on its website: http://www.dti.gov.uk/er/equality/so_rb_longexplan.pdf. This document does not, however, have any legal status, unlike a statutory Code of Practice, although we have quoted from it fairly extensively in this book, representing as it does, the considered views of the drafters of two of the Regulations covered. We have also quoted from two guides for employers and employees published by ACAS: *Religion or Belief and the Workplace* and *Sexual Orientation and the Workplace*.

When it comes to implementing the changes to the Race Relations Act and the Disability Discrimination Act, there is the additional issue of non-regression. Thus, Article 6(2) of the Race Discrimination Directive provides: 'The implementation of this Directive shall under no circumstances constitute grounds for a reduction in the level of protection against discrimination already afforded by Member States in the fields covered by the Directive.' This is the principle of non-regression and in the case of the Race Relations Act 1976, there are several changes that may not comply with this fundamental requirement:

- The definition of racial harassment by including an objective dimension that may take account of the motive of the putative harasser arguably makes it more difficult for a complainant to establish their case than under the provisions of the Race Relations Act 1976 before their amendment. The same issue may arise under the DDA.
- The generalised genuine occupational requirement exception may allow the exclusion of someone on grounds of race, ethnic or national origin in circumstances in which such an exclusion would not have operated under

the narrowly-drawn genuine occupational qualifications in the Race Relations Act.

Because the Government chose to implement the Directives by Regulations, there is also no comprehensive single Equality Act. The result is not only inconsistency, but also the creation of a hierarchy of oppression. Those discriminated against on grounds of race are protected both in terms of employment discrimination and discrimination as regards access to goods, facilities and services. There is a statutory enforcement commission. Moreover, there is a duty on public authorities not to discriminate on grounds of race in carrying out their functions and to promote racial equality. Those discriminated against on grounds of disability will be in the same position, when a public authority duty is imposed via the draft Disability Bill, which is expected to become law in 2005. There is no current Government commitment to introducing such a duty as regards equality between women and men, but the protection against discrimination on grounds of sex also includes non-employment issues. As for those discriminated against on grounds of religion or belief or on grounds of sexual orientation, the legislation does not apply outside the field of employment and vocational training, there is no statutory agency with enforcement and promotional powers, and there is no special duty on public authorities.

In time, it is likely that these anomalies will be rectified. A single enforcement agency, a Commission for Equality and Human Rights, is on the cards for 2006, in time for the new jurisdiction of age discrimination as well. It seems unlikely at the moment that the legislation setting up the new Commission will also incorporate a single Equality Act. Instead, we can expect the Government to ask the new Commission to examine this as one of its initial priorities and to make recommendations. That would mean that there would not be a single Equality Act in force before the next decade.

These problems of implementation are regrettable, but they should not obscure the central message of the new Regulations, and of this book: workers have been given important new rights not to be discriminated against on grounds of religion or belief, or sexual orientation, and the rights not to be discriminated against on grounds of race and disability have been made more effective. Employers, and those who advise them, will need to understand how the Regulations will affect policies and procedures, and will need to keep abreast of how the Regulations are being interpreted by the tribunals and appellate courts.

The aim of this report is to pick out the key parts of this new legislation, especially those aspects of wider interest and of practical importance. It does not aim to be a fully comprehensive guide.

Finally, I would like to thank my wife, Bar, and my daughter, Holly, for their patience with many disrupted evenings and weekends. I would not recommend undertaking this sort of project to anyone seeking to obtain a better work-life balance.

Michael Rubenstein

March 2004

Cross-strand issues

Direct discrimination

The definition of direct discrimination is essentially the same as regards race discrimination, religious discrimination and sexual orientation discrimination. There are different definitions for disability discrimination and this is dealt with in Part II of the book.

The definition of direct discrimination provides:

'a person ("A") discriminates against another person ("B") if –
(a) on grounds of [religion or belief/sexual orientation/race], A treats B less favourably then he treats or would treat other persons.'

This introduces the concept of 'A' and 'B' found in various parts of all the new discrimination Regulations. 'A' is a bad person who always discriminates (or at least gets accused of it), whereas poor 'B' always gets discriminated against.

Other than the introduction of 'A' and 'B', there is no substantive difference between the old definition of direct discrimination in the Race Relations Act and the new one. The definition is also similar to that in the Sex Discrimination Act 1975, s 1.

This means that unlike some of the new EU-based rights such as the Part-Time Workers Regulations and the Fixed-term Employees Regulations, direct discrimination – discrimination on the particular ground in question – cannot be justified by an employer under these Regulations. If an employer discriminates against someone on grounds of their race, or their religion or their sexual orientation, that will be automatically unlawful, unless the case falls within one of the narrowly-drawn genuine occupational requirements.

Comparable circumstances

The new Regulations provide that:

'a comparison of B's case with that of another person ... must be such that the relevant circumstances in the one case are the same, or not materially different, in the other.'

In order to prove direct discrimination, therefore, the applicant must compare his or her treatment with the treatment that was or would be afforded to a comparator in circumstances that are the same, or not materially different. From an applicant's standpoint, the importance of identifying a comparator whose circumstances are comparable was highlighted by the decision of the House of Lords in *Shamoon v Chief Constable of the Royal Ulster Constabulary* [2003] UKHL 11, [2003] IRLR 285, HL. In that case, a police officer's claim of sex discrimination in respect of a decision to take away the function of writing staff appraisals from her was ultimately unsuccessful because there were held to be material differences between the circumstances relating to the male police officers she compared herself with that ruled out their use as comparators. The DTI explanatory notes adapt the facts of *Shamoon* to a religious discrimination context to make this point:'it would not be direct discrimination on grounds of religion or belief if a Jewish employee were no longer permitted to write staff reports after complaints were made about her reporting technique, if the employer would have stopped any employee against whom such complaints were made from writing reports, regardless of their religion.'

From the standpoint of employers and those advising them, the great advantage of an argument that there are material differences between the circumstances relating to the applicant and his or her comparators is that, if successful, it will knock out the discrimination claim before the burden of proof shifts to show a non-discriminatory reason. Bear in mind in this context, however, that *Shamoon* also emphasises that if there is no actual comparator whose circumstances are the same, the statutory comparison should be with how a hypothetical comparator in those same circumstances would be treated. The way others are treated whose circumstances are insufficiently similar to be actual comparators then becomes evidence of how a hypothetical comparator in the same circumstances would be treated. See also *Chief Constable of West Yorkshire Police v Vento* [2001] IRLR 124, EAT.

Perceived discrimination

Unlike the definition of direct discrimination in the Sex Discrimination Act, which refers to less favourable treatment on the ground of 'her' sex, the religious discrimination and sexual orientation definitions follow the definition in the Race Relations Act 1976 and merely refer to less favourable treatment 'on grounds of religion or belief' or 'on grounds of sexual orientation'.

This means, in principle, that direct discrimination can be on grounds of the discriminator's perception of a person's sexual orientation, religion or belief, or race, even if that perception is not accurate. This is discussed in more detail in the chapters on religion or belief and on sexual orientation, together with the controversial partial exception to this principle that applies where there is a genuine occupational requirement relating to sexual orientation.

Discrimination by association

The wording of the definition of direct discrimination, by its reference to 'on grounds of', also prohibits discrimination by reason of the race, or religion or belief, or sexual orientation of someone with whom the person discriminated against associates.

So far as race discrimination is concerned, this was established by the decision of the EAT in *Zarczynska v Levy* [1978] IRLR 532, approved per Lord Hope in *Macdonald v Advocate General for Scotland* [2003] UKHL 34, [2003] IRLR 512, HL.

Refusing to follow an instruction to discriminate

In *Weathersfield Ltd v Sargent* [1999] IRLR 94, the Court of Appeal ruled that an employee is unfavourably treated on racial grounds if they are required to carry out a racially discriminatory trading policy, even though the instruction concerns those of a different racial group to that of the complainant. The language of the Regulations on religion or belief and on sexual orientation is the same for this purpose, so this principle will apply.

Burden of proof

All the new Regulations implement the burden of proof provisions in the Race Discrimination and Framework Employment Directives. These parallel the changes made to the Sex Discrimination Act by the Sex Discrimination (Indirect Discrimination and Burden of Proof) Regulations 2001.

The Regulations provide that where a complaint of unlawful discrimination or harassment has been presented to an employment tribunal:

> 'where, on the hearing of the complaint, the complainant proves facts from which the tribunal could ... conclude in the absence of an adequate explanation that the respondent ... has committed ... an act of discrimination or harassment against the complainant ... the tribunal shall uphold the complaint unless the respondent proves that he did not commit ... that act.'

The DTI explanatory notes say that this means that 'once the person making the complaint has made out a prima facie case – in other words, where the tribunal could in the absence of an explanation consider that discrimination or harassment has taken place – it is for the respondent to the complaint (eg the employer) to prove that he did not commit the act of discrimination or harassment.'

This represents a significant shift from the previous race discrimination case law as exemplified by the Court of Appeal's decision in *King v Great Britain-China Centre* [1991] IRLR 513 approved by the House of Lords in *Zafar v Glasgow City Council* [1998] IRLR 36, HL, in that once a prima facie case has been established, the onus shifts to the employer to prove that it did not commit an act of discrimination and, if this onus is not discharged, a tribunal 'shall' – ie must – find that the employer unlawfully discriminated.

Unfortunately, as we shall see, there is considerable uncertainty as to what the changes to the burden of proof mean and considerable misunderstanding by the courts as to their effect. This is despite the fact that the changes as regards sex discrimination have been in force since 12 October 2001 and the new rules relating to the burden of proof in race discrimination cases have operated since 19 July 2003, and in the case of both statutes, the new burden of proof is intended to apply in proceedings that are taking place at the commencement date, rather than to cases where the alleged act of discrimination took place after the commencement date. Indeed, as the Home Office notes on the Race Relations Act (Amendment) Regulations point out, it is only 'cases in which the proceedings were determined before the commencement date' that 'will be unaffected.'

There are, essentially, two separate issues raised by the new wording: when does the burden shift, and what happens when it does shift?

What shifts the burden?

The Regulations adopt the traditional standard of a prima facie case: the complainant must offer evidence that is adequate to create an inference that the act in question was on grounds of race, religion, sexual orientation etc if there was no evidence put forward by the other side. In other words, if the tribunal stopped the case after hearing the applicant's preliminary evidence, without hearing any explanation by the employer, is there sufficient evidence for it to conclude that there was unlawful discrimination?

But how much evidence is required? What are 'facts from which the tribunal could ... conclude in the absence of an adequate explanation that the respondent ... has committed ... an act of discrimination'? This is one of the key areas for the development of discrimination law generally over the next few years.

There is little guidance from the DTI, which says that 'the consideration of the burden of proof and when it shifts from complainant to respondent will depend on the facts of each case.'

Let us imagine a black applicant who unsuccessfully applies for a job. He thinks that this may have been due to his race and brings a complaint of race discrimination. In *Anya v University of Oxford* [2001] EWCA Civ 405, [2001] IRLR 377, CA, Sedley LJ suggested that where there is a selection process, 'it is not unduly onerous ... to proceed from the simple fact of such a choice, if it is accompanied by difference in race, to a request for an explanation.'

Does this mean that all it takes to shift the burden of proof to the employer is for a black person to show that he applied for a job that a white person got? Or is more required, and if so what?

It is certainly arguable that a difference of race (or religion or sexual orientation) does not amount to sufficient facts from which the tribunal could conclude in the absence of an adequate explanation that the employer discriminated on grounds of race. That really would be coming close to treating an employer as guilty until proven innocent.

At a minimum, before the burden shifts to the employer to disprove discrimination, it is likely that tribunals will require the applicant to show that he or she met the stated qualifications for the job.

The law may well go further. Some might think that before a tribunal could presume discrimination, in the absence of an explanation, the applicant should have to show that they not only met the minimum qualifications for the job, but that they were equally or even better qualified than the successful candidate. Support for this view can be derived from the provisions found in all the Regulations and discussed above that the relevant circumstances as between

the applicant's case and that of their comparator must 'the same, or not materially different', and the recent emphasis in the case law, such as *Shamoon v Chief Constable of the Royal Ulster Constabulary*, that like must be compared with like.

What happens when the burden shifts

The Government consistently took the view that the shift in the burden of proof was not of importance (see the Cabinet Office guidance on the 2001 Regulations), but, as noted above, this stance changed when the new Regulations were introduced.

Under the old case law, the test was that set out by Neill LJ in *King v Great Britain-China Centre*: if the tribunal considers the employer's explanation to be inadequate or unsatisfactory it was 'legitimate' for it to infer that the discrimination was on racial grounds, but it did not have to do so. That was the whole point of the *King* case, which disapproved a line of cases culminating in *Chattopadhyay v Headmaster of Holloway School* [1981] IRLR 487, EAT, which suggested that the burden of proof shifted to the employer.

Under the Regulations, once a prima facie case has been established, the onus does shift to the employer to prove that it did not commit an act of discrimination and, if this onus is not discharged, a tribunal 'shall' – ie must – find that the employer unlawfully discriminated. This represents a significant difference. It is a far cry from it being 'legitimate' to draw an inference of discrimination to a tribunal being compelled by statute to draw that inference.

This was recognised by the EAT in *Barton v Investec Henderson Crosthwaite Securities Ltd* [2003] IRLR 332, which considered for the first time the similar language of the Sex Discrimination Act after implementation of the Burden of Proof Regulations. The EAT said: 'To discharge that burden it is necessary for the respondent to prove, on the balance of probabilities, that the treatment was in no sense whatsoever on the grounds of sex, since "no discrimination whatsoever" is compatible with the Burden of Proof Directive ... .That requires a tribunal to assess not merely whether the respondent has proved an explanation for the facts from which such inferences can be drawn, but further that it is adequate to discharge the burden of proof on the balance of probabilities that sex was not any part of the reasons for the treatment in question.' The language of the new Regulations, as mentioned, is similar to the amended Sex Discrimination Act, so the same considerations should apply.

Unfortunately, a certain amount of confusion has been generated by remarks made by Simon Brown LJ in *Nelson v Carillion Services Ltd* [2003] EWCA Civ 544, [2003] IRLR 428, CA. He said: 'It seems to me tolerably clear that the effect of s 63A [the amendment made to the Sex Discrimination Act by the Burden of Proof Regulations] was to codify rather than alter the pre-existing position established by the case law. The burden of proving indirect discrimination was always on the complainant, and there pursuant to s 63A it remains, the complainant still having to prove facts from which the tribunal could conclude that he or she has been unlawfully discriminated against "in the absence of an adequate explanation" from the employer. Unless and until the complainant establishes that the condition in question has had a disproportionate adverse impact upon his/her sex, the tribunal could not in my judgment, even without explanation from the employer, conclude that he or she has been unlawfully discriminated against.'

This passage has been misunderstood by the EAT on several occasions (see, for example, *Hillingdon London Borough v Meek*, UKEAT/0422/03) because the first sentence has been taken out of context. *Nelson v Carillion* was an equal pay case and the issue was one of indirect discrimination, not direct discrimination. When Simon Brown LJ's statement is viewed as a whole, it can be seen that the remarks concerning codification of the case law relate to indirect discrimination only. If they were intended to go further, they are, with respect, incorrect. The change to the Sex Discrimination Act 1975, like the

change made to the Race Relations Act, is intended to alter the pre-existing position established by the case law, insofar as direct discrimination is concerned. The correct position, it is submitted, is that put by the CRE in its advice on the Race Relations Regulations: 'For the discriminator the consequences of the new burden of proof will be significant: any failure to provide a satisfactory or adequate explanation, to comply with Codes of Practice or equivocation in a questionnaire response may be determinative since the courts and tribunal must find in favour of the complainant.'

Victimisation

All the Regulations make it unlawful for an employer to discriminate by way of victimisation. The basic wording used is unchanged so far as the Race Relations and Disability Discrimination Acts are concerned, and similar wording has been adopted in the case of the Religion or Belief and Sexual Orientation Regulations.

The Regulations provide that a person victimises another person if he treats them less favourably than he treats or would treat others in the same circumstances by reason that they have done something under or in connection with the Regulations.

There are thus two ingredients to a victimisation claim. First, the complainant must have taken one of the protected acts listed in the Regulations, such as having brought proceedings under the Regulations, giving evidence or information in connection with proceedings or alleging that a person has contravened the Regulations. Secondly, the employer must have treated the claimant less favourably because they took the protected act.

The protection against victimisation covers allegations that are unfounded, unless the allegation was both false and not made in good faith.

Harassment

All four of the Regulations include a new and freestanding provision that makes harassment on the ground in question specifically unlawful. This is contained in s 3A of the Race Relations Act 1976, as amended, s 3B of the Disability Discrimination Act 1995, as amended, and regs 5 of both the Religion or Belief Regulations and the Sexual Orientation Regulations.

There are two parts to the new definition of harassment. Using the language of reg 5 of the Sexual Orientation Regulations, the first part provides:

'(1) For the purposes of these Regulations, a person ("A") subjects another person ("B") to harassment where, on the grounds of sexual orientation, A engages in unwanted conduct which has the purpose or effect of –

(a) violating B's dignity, or

(b) creating an intimidating, hostile, degrading, humiliating or offensive environment for B.'

Unwanted conduct

The first limb of sub-s (1) emphasises that what is at issue is conduct that is 'unwanted' by the recipient. This is consistent with the pioneering European Commission Code of Practice on measures to combat sexual harassment at work and the case law under the Sex Discrimination and Race Relations Acts. Conduct that is not unwanted – that is freely entered into – can never be harassive in terms of the law, though it may contravene an employer's own policies.

Whether conduct is unwanted or not, however, may be difficult to determine in practice. The legal test derives from that relating to sexual harassment, where UK law has rightly recognised that consensual sexual conduct, such as flirtatious behaviour and even consensual touching, cannot be regarded as harassment. The same considerations are unlikely to apply as regards racial harassment and harassment based on disability, religion or sexual orientation. It is highly unlikely that a Pakistani subjected at work to racist or Islamaphobic jokes, for example, will truly welcome this conduct, whatever their overt reaction to it. Failure to object, or even responding with jokes of a similar ilk, is much more likely to be due to a reluctance to protest.

There is no principle, therefore, that harassive conduct should not be regarded as 'unwanted' unless formal objection has been taken to it. As the EAT made clear in *Reed v Stedman* [1999] IRLR 299, there is some conduct that must be assumed to be unwelcome until otherwise proved to the contrary. Racist and homophobic remarks, religious slurs, and remarks demeaning to disabled persons should be regarded as falling within this category.

Proof

Note that to fall within whichever of the relevant Regulations, the conduct in question must be on one of the grounds prohibited by the Regulations: ie it is not enough for an applicant to show that they have been bullied and that they are a Hindu; they must show that they have been bullied on grounds that they are a Hindu.

On the other hand, the definition of harassment is freestanding in the sense that in order to succeed a complainant does not have to identify a comparator of a different race, religion etc who has been treated less favourably. It is sufficient to establish the conduct, its purpose or effect, and whether it is on the prohibited ground. To that extent, the compulsory comparison between the treatment of a woman and the treatment of a man laid down by the House of Lords in *Macdonald v Advocate General for Scotland* [2003] UKHL 34, [2003] IRLR 512, HL in cases of sexual harassment does not apply to cases under the new Regulations.

Moreover, the provisions relating to the reversal of the burden of proof (see Chapter 1) will operate in the case of a claim of unlawful harassment. Thus, for example, proof of race-specific offensive remarks will suffice to establish a prima facie case of harassment shifting the burden to the employer to prove that the conduct was not on grounds of race or was not otherwise unlawful.

Purpose or effect

The first limb of the definition of harassment in the Regulations also provides that unwanted conduct can be unlawful either where it is intentionally harassive or, even if it does not have that purpose, where it has the requisite effect, as defined in sub-s (1)(a) or (b).

This is a potentially important distinction because reg 5(2), as discussed below, goes on to set out a test of reasonableness in judging whether particular conduct could be said to have violated an employee's dignity or created an intimidating, hostile, degrading, humiliating or offensive environment.

Where it can be shown that the conduct in question had this 'purpose', no test applies of whether the employee was reasonable in so regarding it. The practical issue here is whether conduct that is repeated after it has been made clear that it is unwanted then will be regarded as having the requisite purpose. Take the case of a man whose religious views are such that he is made uncomfortable by overhearing discussion of sexual experiences. He is recruited for a job in a workplace where this kind of discussion takes place from time to time. He makes known his objections, which are resented by some of the other employees, who have enjoyed this kind of banter and regard the religious employee's objections as unreasonable. If the employees persist in the behaviour in the presence of the religious employee, knowing that he finds it objectionable, that may lead to a finding that the 'purpose' of the conduct was to violate the employee's dignity or create an offensive working environment for him. If so, it will be automatically unlawful, regardless of the actual effect on the employee or, more significantly, the reasonableness of the employee's reaction to the conduct.

The lesson is that an employer may be legally liable for harassment that is persisted in after the employee has indicated that the conduct is unwanted. It is not decisive for this purpose whether the indication that the conduct was unwanted was made to the employer or to the employees concerned, since all the Regulations specifically provide that an employer can be held liable for the acts of its employees done in the course of employment, whether or not it knew or approved of them, unless the employer can show that it took such steps as were reasonably practicable to prevent its employee from doing the discriminatory act. Employers will need to ensure that this is reflected in their harassment policies. Once a complaint of harassment has been made by an employee, even if an employer thinks that the complaint is unreasonable, it will have to be very careful as to how the complaint is dealt with. If the employer allows the conduct to be repeated, it will risk a finding that the reason why it was repeated was to violate the employee's dignity or create an offensive working environment for them.

Dignity and working environment

The two subsections distinguish between the individual's 'dignity' and their working environment. The Framework Employment and Race Discrimination Directives require both to be affected, but the Government considered, rightly, that to incorporate such a standard into UK discrimination law would be regressive in comparison with the test currently employed by tribunals in cases of racial (and sexual) harassment. Thus, proof of either element will suffice to establish unlawful harassment. For example, a one-off incident of homophobic harassment might be said to violate the recipient's dignity without it creating an offensive working environment, which implies something of greater breadth and duration than a one-off incident. Conversely, an employer who tolerated homophobic remarks in the workplace might be said to have created an offensive working environment for gay people, even if the applicant was unable to point to a remark specifically directed to them as an individual, which violated their dignity.

In order for unwanted conduct to have the requisite effect on the working environment, it is sufficient that it can be characterised as either having created an 'intimidating', or a 'hostile', or a 'degrading', or a 'humiliating' or an 'offensive' working environment for the employee. Only one element needs to be established.

Objective test

Regulation 5(2) goes on to provides that:

> 'conduct shall be regarded as having the effect specified in para 1(a) or (b) only if, having regard to all the circumstances, including in particular the perception of B, it should reasonably be considered as having that effect.'

This part of the Regulation adds an objective dimension to the test of harassment in cases where it cannot be established that the harasser had a discriminatory purpose. In principle, it is the necessary counterpart to the definition of harassment as a subjective concept. It is for the recipient to determine whether the conduct is 'unwanted' by her or him. Whether the conduct has the effect of violating the recipient's dignity depends on how they, subjectively, perceive the conduct, as does whether the conduct has the effect of creating a degrading or offensive environment for them. It is for each person to determine what offends them. Yet, since legal rights and liability are at issue, it is simply commonsense to place some objective parameters on this subjective concept. Otherwise, in effect, an employer could be liable for unlawful 'harassment' no matter how unreasonable a recipient's perception of behaviour was.

The Regulation expressly instructs the tribunal to take into account the perception of the applicant as one of the circumstances in deciding whether it was reasonable for the applicant to consider that their dignity was violated or that an offensive working environment had been created by the conduct in question. The question is what are the other circumstances that are relevant? One might make a case for saying it covers harassment that is genuinely inadvertent. The example of Coleman Silk, the college professor in Philip Roth's *The Human Stain*, comes to mind. He was brought up on harassment charges when he inquired about two students who had never attended his class, 'are they spooks?', without realising that the students concerned were black and that this had a derogatory meaning for black people.

Most of the other possible circumstances that a tribunal might take into account in this context, however, are highly controversial, such as the perception or motive of the harasser, the nature of the workplace, and whether the employer knew of the religion, sexual orientation, disability etc of the complainant.

Thus, the DTI explanatory notes say: 'The fact that an employer might be unaware of an employee's sexual orientation or religious belief may be a relevant factor to be taken into account when considering the effect of the conduct in a case.'

This appears questionable. Suppose an employer makes an anti-Semitic comment to a Jewish employee, without knowing that the employee is Jewish. The employer's lack of awareness certainly would be a relevant factor when considering the purpose of the conduct, but it is hard to see its relevance for determining whether the effect of the remark should reasonably be considered as having violated the employee's dignity. Indeed, the message given out by the DTI's statement here is somewhat distasteful, since it conjures up the image of the bigoted employer who stops telling jokes that are offensive when particular employees walk into the room.

Harassment by employers and others

Accompanying the freestanding definition of harassment are provisions that make it unlawful for an employer 'to subject to harassment a person whom he employs or who has applied to him for employment'.

All the new Regulations make it unlawful for a principal to subject a contract worker to harassment. This means that temporary workers employed by an agency have as much right to be protected against harassment as the client's own workers. For example, an employer cannot assume that it does not matter if a worker is offended by religious or homophobic remarks because the worker is only a temporary. The agency worker whose dignity is violated or who is subjected to an offensive working environment could bring a claim under the contract worker provisions.

The Regulations also made it unlawful for a trade union, employers' organisation or similar trade organisation to subject its members, or applicants for membership, to harassment.

The definitions of discrimination by a qualifications body, by providers of vocational training, by employment agencies, and providers of careers services also make it unlawful to subject a person to harassment in connection with their respective functions.

Third party harassment

For many years, the decision of the EAT in *Burton v De Vere Hotels Ltd* [1996] IRLR 596 provided a valuable framework for dealing with third party racial or sexual harassment. The case involved a claim by two black waitresses that they had experienced harassment as a result of working at a dinner addressed by Bernard Manning. They were not harassed either by a manager or by a fellow employee, so the traditional rules relating to employer liability for workplace discrimination did not apply. Nevertheless, the EAT held that the employer was legally liable.

It was clear that the two waitresses had been subjected to degrading treatment. The EAT set out the principle that an employer subjects an employee to the detriment of harassment if it permitted the harassment to occur in circumstances in which it could control whether it happens or not.

This was the law until the decision of the House of Lords in *Pearce v Governing Body of Mayfield Secondary School* [2003] UKHL 34, [2003] IRLR 512, HL, the case of homophobic abuse of a lesbian teacher by pupils in the school. The employment tribunal held in the alternative that if the abuse of the applicant by school pupils had been on grounds of sex, the school would have been directly liable for the discrimination in accordance with the test laid down in the Bernard Manning case. When the case got to the House of Lords, it made a point of ruling that the Bernard Manning case was wrongly decided. This was because it was not sufficient to find that the waitresses had been racially abused. In order for the employer to be legally liable, the House of Lords said that it also had to be shown that the employer had put the waitresses in that position because of their race. The tribunal's finding that the hotel manager's failure to protect the waitresses from the offensive content of the comedian's speech was not connected with their ethnic origin, and that, by implication, the employer would have treated white waitresses in the same way, negatived racial discrimination on the part of the employer.

The House of Lords' decision is relevant for all the new Regulations to the extent that it clearly suggests that an employer can be liable for subjecting an employee to the detriment of being put in the position where they were harassed by a third party only if it can be shown both that the situation was under the employer's control and the employer put the employee in that position, or failed to prevent the harassment from occurring because of the employee's race, religion or belief, sexual orientation or disability. This means that they have to show that if they were of a different race, religion etc and were harassed by a third party, they would have been treated more favourably, such as by preventative steps being taken. So if, for example, the employer treats third party sexual harassment of heterosexual women more seriously than sexual harassment of lesbians, there would be less favourable treatment of a lesbian on grounds of sexual orientation. However, if the employer treats all third party harassment in the same way, such as by ignoring it, there would be no unlawful harassment within the meaning of the Regulations as currently interpreted, if an employee is subjected to harassment by someone for whom the employer is not legally responsible. The DTI explanatory notes provide a stark example: 'an employer who runs a shop would not be liable for insulting remarks made to one of his gay employees by a customer, except in the event that the reason why the employer failed to prevent the harassment was because the employee was gay.'

The House of Lords' comments disapproving *Burton v DeVere* were observations not necessary for determining the case and, strictly speaking, not binding on lower courts and tribunals. The *Pearce* case itself in which the remarks were made was decided on the special facts of harassment of a teacher by school children, and their Lordships were clearly concerned about the limits a school has in controlling the behaviour of its pupils. Coming from our highest court, obviously the remarks are of the greatest weight, but it also has to be said that the disapproval of the Bernard Manning case has caused concern in the lower ranks of the judiciary and has been widely criticised by commentators.

Consider the DTI's example of the employee who is put in a position in which they are being harassed by a customer on grounds of their sexual orientation. They complain about it to their employer, but suppose that the employer says that they will have to put up with it or leave because the customer is too important commercially. If the case came to a tribunal, the fact that the employee complained about third party harassment on grounds of their sexual orientation and that the employer did nothing about it is likely to be regarded as sufficient to establish a prima facie case of discrimination shifting the burden of proof to the employer to show that it did not discriminate on grounds of sexual orientation. This could only be done via a 'bastard' defence – that the employer would ignore all complaints of harassment by this customer, whatever their grounds – and tribunals rightly will require proof of this by the employer, not merely an assertion. One suspects that tribunals will strive to find a remedy for employees subjected to third party harassment, and that employers in such a position will be advised to think very carefully before using such a defence.

It is also interesting in this connection to look at the language of the Directives in this context. Taking the language of the Framework Directive, it defines harassment as follows:

> 'Harassment shall be deemed to be discrimination within the meaning of para 1, when unwanted conduct related to any of the grounds referred to in Article 1 takes place with the purpose or effect of violating the dignity of a person and of creating an intimidating, hostile, degrading, humiliating or offensive environment. In this context, the concept of harassment may be defined in accordance with the national laws and practices of the Member States.'

This suggests that if harassment takes place with the requisite effect on the employee or their working environment, it *shall* be regarded as contrary to the Directive. The courts may take the view that the remarks concerning third party harassment of an employee while at work may require revisiting in light of this broad language.

Employers faced with complaints of third party harassment should also bear in mind that liability under discrimination law for third party discrimination is not necessarily coterminous with liability under health and safety and personal injury law. An employer who does nothing about the complaint of an employee who is subjected to harassment on grounds that they are not legally responsible for the harasser may find themselves defending a personal injury claim based on the psychiatric injury to the employee that resulted.

Detriment not harassment

Harassment was not specifically unlawful under sex, race and disability discrimination legislation. It was only unlawful because it was accepted by the courts as subjecting the employee concerned to a 'detriment'.

Now harassment is made specifically unlawful. As a result, the definitions section in the Race Relations Act (Amendment) Regulations explicitly states that 'detriment' does not include 'conduct of a nature such as to constitute harassment under s 3A'. The

definitions section in the Disability Discrimination Act (Amendment) Regulations says that '"detriment" does not include conduct of the nature referred to in s 3B (harassment).' The definitions section in the Regulations on discrimination on grounds of religion or belief and on grounds of sexual orientation state that 'detriment' does not include harassment within the meaning of reg 5.

This is an anti-overlap limitation, presumably regarded as necessary by the Government because the standard of proof is considerably lower under existing case law to establish a 'detriment' than it is under the freestanding definition of harassment, where a number of ingredients have to be satisfied in order for a claim to be successful.

The wording of all the anti-overlap provisions, however, appears peculiar. The test for what is a detriment was most recently set out by the House of Lords in *Shamoon v Chief Constable of the Royal Ulster Constabulary* [2003] UKHL 11, [2003] IRLR 285, HL. According to the House of Lords, in order for a disadvantage to qualify as a 'detriment', the court or tribunal must find that by reason of the act or acts complained of a reasonable worker would or might take the view that he had thereby been disadvantaged in the circumstances in which he had thereafter to work. This seems a less stringent test than the new test for harassment. It appears conceivable that someone could experience behaviour related to race or religion or disability or sexual orientation that places them at a disadvantage without it meeting one of the elements required for a freestanding claim of harassment, for example that the conduct was insufficiently severe so as to be said to violate their dignity or create a working environment that can be characterised as intimidating, hostile, degrading, humiliating or offensive.

In those circumstances, read literally, the conduct complained of would not fall within the statutory definition of harassment, so the anti-overlap provisions would not apply at all, and the employee would seem to be free to label their claim as detrimental treatment. Indeed, the definition in the Race Relations (Amendment) Regulations specifically states that 'this section does not affect the law relating to harassment – (a) in circumstances other than those referred to in subsection (1)', sub-s (1) being the aforementioned definition of harassment. For this reason, it would seem that harassment complainants might wish to frame their claim in the alternative: 'I have been unlawfully harassed, but if you find that the conduct was not harassment, I submit that it was detrimental treatment.'

Indirect discrimination

The law relating to indirect discrimination requires an employer to justify policies or practices applied to all groups, but which have an adverse impact on those of a particular group. The legal standard for proving indirect discrimination under the new Regulations is likely to be considerably easier for applicants to satisfy than the old test under the Sex Discrimination and Race Relations Acts.

Article 2(2)(b) of the Framework Employment Directive stipulates that indirect discrimination shall be taken to occur where:

> 'an apparently neutral provision, criterion or practice would put persons having a particular religion or belief, a particular disability, a particular age, or a particular sexual orientation at a particular disadvantage compared with other persons unless: (i) that provision, criterion or practice is objectively justified by a legitimate aim and the means of achieving that aim are appropriate and necessary ....'

The Race Discrimination Directive uses similar language in respect of persons of a 'racial or ethnic origin'.

In accordance with the Government's commitment to adopting a coherent approach to discrimination across equality legislation, the definition of indirect discrimination used for race, religion or belief, and sexual orientation in the new Regulations is similar (disability discrimination is not covered by the new definition). However, the definition does not directly transpose the language of the Directives. Instead, using the language of reg 3(1)(b) of the Religion or Belief Regulations, indirect discrimination is defined as:

> 'a person ("A") discriminates against another person ("B") if ... A applies to B a provision, criterion or practice which he applies or would apply equally to persons not of the same religion or belief as B, but –

(i)   which puts or would put persons of the same religion or belief as B at a particular disadvantage when compared with other persons,

(ii) which puts B at that disadvantage, and

(iii) which A cannot show to be a proportionate means of achieving a legitimate aim.'

Scope

The first limb of this definition, like the Sex Discrimination Act following implementation of the Sex Discrimination (Indirect Discrimination and Burden of Proof) Regulations 2001, makes clear that a 'provision, criterion or practice' can be challenged. This is a much broader concept than a 'requirement or condition', as found in the former test in the Race Relations Act 1976, s 1(1)(b) because it covers informal workplace practices as well as formal ones.

Establishing group disadvantage

The language of the Sex Discrimination and Race Relations Acts as first enacted stipulated that an indirect discrimination complainant had to establish that a requirement or condition was such that a 'considerably smaller' proportion of their group could comply with it than the proportion of their comparator group who could comply. This often resulted in complex arguments as to what is 'considerably smaller' and how it was to be proven.

Regulation 3(1)(b)(i) of both the Religion and Sexual Orientation Regulations, by its reference to a provision, criterion or practice that puts or 'would put' a group at a disadvantage, suggests that detailed statistical evidence as to the impact of the challenged practice may not always be necessary. This was certainly in the minds of the Council of the EU when the Framework Directive was adopted. Recital 15 to this states:

'The appreciation of the facts from which it may be inferred that there has been direct or indirect discrimination is a matter for national judicial or other competent bodies, in accordance with rules of national law or practice. Such rules may provide, in particular, for indirect discrimination to be established by any means including on the basis of statistical evidence.'

Although an argument can be put that UK national practice does require disparate impact to be established via statistical evidence, the better view is that the test is intended to be more flexible and that these often arid statistical comparisons are no longer necessary. It should be sufficient if it can be shown, perhaps via economic or sociological evidence, that the practice would be likely to have an adverse impact on the group to which the applicant belongs. This could cover practices that are well-known as 'tending' to discriminate against minority groups, such as word-of-mouth recruitment.

The more flexible approach will be important, both as regards religious and sexual orientation discrimination, where reliable statistics as to numbers affected in a particular workplace by a practice may not be available. It might be possible to establish group disadvantage simply by adducing documentary evidence. For example, the *ACAS Guide to the Religious Discrimination Regulations* says that 'if team meetings always take place on a Friday afternoon this may discriminate against Jewish and Muslim staff for whom Friday afternoon has a particular religious significance, although not everyone follows their faith in the same way.' If an observant Muslim brought an indirect religious discrimination claim complaining that they had been disadvantaged because they were unable to attend Friday afternoon team meetings, it might well be open to him to establish at least a presumption that this practice has an adverse impact simply by quoting this portion of the ACAS Guide.

The phrase 'puts or would put' is broader in one further sense. It allows policies or practices to be challenged at an early stage before they have had much impact on the particular complainants.

The effect of these changes, therefore, is to put the focus much more on whether the provision, criterion or practice is justifiable.

Individual disadvantage

The definition of indirect discrimination in the Directives, quoted above, refers merely to a provision, criterion or practice that 'would put' persons at a disadvantage. However, the Regulations stipulate that the provision, criterion or practice must be one that actually 'puts' the applicant at the disadvantage. This, like the definitions in the previous legislation, confirms that hypothetical cases cannot be brought. The practice must, in fact, disadvantage the applicant or applicants challenging it. Although the new definition uses the word 'disadvantage' rather than 'detriment', this is a distinction without a difference as 'detriment' has been interpreted as meaning 'placing under a disadvantage'. Is the difference from the wording in the Directives significant? To the extent that it simply means that individuals must have legal standing to bring a complaint, this can be regarded as a national procedural rule unaffected by the Directive. But to the extent that this language in the Regulations requires a provision, criterion or practice to have already been applied to the individual concerned and would not allow an anticipatory complaint, it would appear not to implement the Directives correctly.

The other change in the wording from the terminology previously used in the Race Relations Act and in the Sex Discrimination Act is that there is no longer a reference to the practice being to the applicant's detriment 'because he cannot comply with it'. Those words sometimes led to a restrictive ruling that an applicant could comply with a requirement, but chose not to do so: most notably in sex discrimination cases where applicants lost their claim that it was indirectly discriminatory not to allow them to return to work part-time after maternity leave, because they had (or were able to afford) child care.

In *Nelson v Carillion Services Ltd* [2003] EWCA Civ 544, [2003] IRLR 428, CA, the Court of Appeal held that the burden is on the applicant to establish the three elements of the first half of the test of indirect discrimination: viz, application of the provision to them; particular disadvantage to members of their group; and personal disadvantage because of membership of that group. The burden then shifts to the employer to justify the provision as 'a proportionate means of achieving a legitimate aim.' It has been argued that this is not the right interpretation of the new burden of proof provisions and that, correctly understood, if the applicant is able to adduce some evidence of a policy's disparate impact, perhaps evidence that it operated to his or her personal disadvantage, the evidential burden should shift to the employer to show that this was not to the disadvantage of the particular group that the applicant is asserting has been disadvantaged. If correct, that would imply that where there are multiple elements for proving discrimination, the burden can shift not just as between the elements but within them. That may be taking the burden of proof rules too far, but the argument is likely to be run at some point or another.

Test of justification

Whether an indirectly discriminatory practice will be lawful or unlawful will depend on whether the employer can show that it is 'a proportionate means of achieving a legitimate aim.'

This language is used to implement the requirement in the Directive that the provision, criterion or practice must be shown to be objectively justified by a legitimate aim and that 'the means of achieving that aim are appropriate and necessary'. The word 'necessary' appeared to be the fly in the ointment as far as the Government was concerned. They were anxious that tribunals would impose a very strict standard of necessity on employers who adopt indirectly discriminatory practices.

There are two limbs to the new statutory test: first, the provision, criterion or practice must pursue a 'legitimate aim', and secondly, it must be a 'proportionate means' of doing so.

A 'legitimate aim' is likely to be interpreted widely, as including interests of the business and administrative efficiency. The DTI notes suggest: 'This may include aims such as effective use of human or other resources, profitability, or administrative efficiency. Market forces dictating that certain workers are in short supply may also be a legitimate aim when paying those jobs more.' Note, however, that the European Court of Justice has recently said on several occasions that cost, in itself, is not a justification. Thus, in *Kutz-Bauer v Freie und Hansestadt Hamburg* [2003] IRLR 368, the ECJ held that an employer cannot justify discrimination solely because avoidance of such discrimination would involve increased costs.

What is less clear is how the test of proportionality will be interpreted. The concept of proportionality is frequently used by the European Court of Human Rights in cases under Article 14, the nondiscrimination article of the European Convention. In such cases, because it is Government laws and practices that are under challenge, the ECHR applies the principle that those accused of indirectly discriminating are entitled to a 'margin of appreciation'. If employers are to be given a 'margin of appreciation' in imposing indirectly discriminatory policies and practices, that would mean that the test would be considerably less stringent than suggested by the Directive (and, in the case of race discrimination, impermissibly regressive).

The DTI takes the view, however, in its explanatory notes that for a practice to be 'proportionate', it must be 'appropriate and necessary'. This is not surprising, since that is the test required by the Directives and any less stringent standard would put the UK in breach of its obligation to implement the Directives correctly. The DTI goes on to say: 'generally, an appropriate means is one that is suitable to achieve the aim in question, and that actually does so. A necessary means is one without which the aim could not be achieved; it is not simply a convenient means. This will include consideration of whether the aim could be achieved by other means that have lesser discriminatory effects.'

Compare this test to the standard set out by the Court of Appeal in *Hampson v Department of Education and Science* [1989] IRLR 69 and approved by the House of Lords in *Webb v EMO Air Cargo (UK) Ltd* [1993] IRLR 27: an objective balance between the discriminatory effect of the requirement or condition and the reasonable needs of the person who applies it. Or the test as most recently expressed by Lord Bingham for the Privy Council in *Tengur v Bishop of Roman Catholic Diocese of Port Louis* [2004] UKPC 9, [2004] All ER (D) 24 (Feb), PC (albeit not in an indirect discrimination context): 'where apparently discriminatory treatment is shown, it is for the alleged discriminator to justify it as having a legitimate aim and as having a reasonable relationship of proportionality between the means employed and the aim sought to be realised.'

The test in the Regulations appears considerably stricter since it focuses on necessity and not reasonableness. To the extent that it focuses on whether the employer could have achieved its aim by other less discriminatory means, it suggests a duty of reasonable accommodation such as is expressly found under US religious discrimination law.

If the Regulations are interpreted by the tribunals in this way, it will make it considerably more difficult for employers to justify indirectly discriminatory practices than was hitherto the case under race and sex discrimination legislation.

The practical lesson is that prudent employers will be reviewing their policies and practices to ascertain whether they operate to the disadvantage of any racial, religious or belief group, or those of a protected sexual orientation. They will then wish to assess whether the justification for the policy or practice is defendable as being a proportionate means for achieving a legitimate aim.

Scope of the legislation

The Race Discrimination and Framework Employment Directives are very widely drawn, admitting of few exceptions from their scope. As a result, the new Regulations are drawn broadly and changes have had to be made to the Race Relations and Disability Discrimination Acts expanding their coverage.

Employment at an establishment in Great Britain

All the Regulations apply only to employment 'at an establishment in Great Britain'. The circumstances in which employment (or contract work) is to be regarded as being at an establishment in Great Britain, however, is very much a term of art.

First of all, the Regulations define an employee's employment as regarded as being at an establishment in Great Britain if the employee 'does his work wholly or partly in Great Britain'. This means that the Regulations treat an employee as employed at an establishment in Great Britain if he or she works partly in Great Britain, even if they only work in Great Britain for a small proportion of their time, and work most of the time overseas.

Even where the employee does his or her work wholly outside Great Britain, they may be treated as employed in Great Britain, and therefore as protected against discrimination on grounds of race, ethnic or national origin, disability, religion or belief, or sexual orientation, provided that:

'(a) the employer has a place of business at an establishment in Great Britain;

(b) the work is for the purposes of the business carried on at that establishment, and

(c) the employee is ordinarily resident in Great Britain (i) at the time he applies for or is offered the employment, or (ii) at any time during the course of the employment.'

The first two criteria mean that in order to be covered by the Regulations, if an employee works wholly outside Great Britain, the employer must have an office in Great Britain and the employee's work must be for the purposes of that office.

If those criteria are met, the employee must be 'ordinarily resident' in Great Britain either at the time they apply for or are offered the job, or at some time during the course of the employment. 'Ordinarily resident' is a tax term, which means resident in Great Britain 'year after year'. (For tax purposes, a person is 'resident' in the UK, if they spend at least half the tax year in the UK, or if they spend at least three months per tax year in the UK on average. They may be resident in the UK if they spend less time in the UK, but they will not be resident if they have not been in the UK at all during the tax year.) According to the DTI explanatory notes: 'The fact that a person goes abroad for long periods at a time may not detract from the fact that they remain ordinarily resident in Britain – for example, if the person keeps their main residence in Britain. Equally, if a person lives from year to year in another country, he is not ordinarily resident in Britain simply by virtue of working temporarily in Britain for a few weeks or months.' The DTI points out that the criteria in the Regulations are 'broadly similar' to those that apply to whether an employee working wholly outside Great Britain may be liable to pay British income tax, 'so if an employee pays income tax in Britain because he is ordinarily resident in Britain, that will provide an indication that the employee is probably caught by reg 9(2).'

The following example is given by the DTI: 'a company in Britain might open a customer service call centre in Ireland to handle its incoming telephone calls from customers. The work done in the centre is for the purposes of the business in Britain, so would meet the first part of the test in reg 9(2). If staff for the centre were recruited in Britain, where they were ordinarily resident, and transferred out to Ireland to work in the centre, they would fall under reg 9(2). However, if staff for the centre were recruited locally in Ireland, they would not fall under reg 9(2) because they were not ordinarily resident in Britain when recruited, or when working at the call centre.'

Specific provision is made in the Regulations in relation to employment on ships, aircraft and hovercraft and for employment on oil and gas rigs.

The central implication of the rules relating to work outside Great Britain is that they will confer rights under the discrimination Regulations on British employees temporarily posted to other parts of the world. This means that such employees will have the right not to be discriminated against on grounds of race, ethnic or national origin, religion or belief, disability or sexual orientation while they are working for their employer overseas and that they will have a remedy against their employer in a British employment tribunal if they are discriminated against.

The standard set out by the new discrimination Regulations is markedly different from the territorial jurisdiction of employment tribunals to hear claims brought under the Employment Rights Act 1996, as interpreted by the Court of Appeal in *Lawson v Serco Ltd* [2004] EWCA Civ 12, [2004] IRLR 206. That case followed the repeal of the exclusion from statutory rights such as unfair dismissal 'where under the employee's contract of employment he ordinarily works outside Great Britain.' The Court of Appeal rejected an expansive view and held that the right not to be unfairly dismissed applies to dismissal from 'employment in Great Britain'.

Office holders

A new provision relating to office holders prohibits discrimination against workers who are not legally in employment but whose position may be similar to that of employees. It applies to:

'(a) any office or post to which persons are appointed to discharge functions personally under the direction of another person, and in respect of which they are entitled to remuneration; and

(b) any office or post to which appointments are made by (or on the recommendation of or subject to the approval of) a Minister of the Crown, a government department, the National Assembly for Wales or any part of the Scottish Administration.'

This means that if the officer holder or post holder is a Government appointment, or is in a position similar to an employee, they will fall within the Regulations.

Examples given by the DTI of the public appointments covered include 'the chairs/members of some non-departmental public bodies, judges and members of tribunals.' However, appointments to political offices are not covered. Nor are elected posts, such as a Member of Parliament.

Previously, the Race Relations and Disability Discrimination Acts applied only where the appointment was made by a Minister of the Crown or a Government department. Moreover, whereas complaints of discrimination in respect of public appointments previously were heard in the civil courts, they will now be heard by employment tribunals.

The Regulations mean that those applying to become members or chairmen of employment tribunals, and those who already sit in such a capacity, will be able to complain if they consider that they have been discriminated against directly or indirectly, or harassed, on grounds of race, religion or belief, sexual orientation, or disability. We discuss the implications of this in further detail in the chapter on disability discrimination.

Contract workers

All the new Regulations make it unlawful for a principal to subject a contract worker to discrimination or harassment. In the case of the Race

Relations and Disability Discrimination Acts, this has entailed modifying existing provisions.

A 'contract worker' is a person who provides services for another person ('the principal') under a contract made between that person and the worker's employer, such as an employment agency. A typical example is a temporary secretary, but the definition of contract worker can include any person loaned or seconded under a contract between one employer and another.

The Regulations place contract workers in a similar position in relation to the principal as that of employees in relation to their employer, and make it unlawful for the principal to discriminate against, or harass, a contract worker.

The DTI explanatory notes give the following as an example: 'a nurse is employed by an agency which supplies staff to a number of hospitals. If, while working in one of the hospitals, the nurse suffers harassment from the hospital's manager, he may bring a complaint against the hospital and against the manager ... '.

In a recent decision under the comparable contract worker provisions of the Sex Discrimination (Northern Ireland) Order, *Jones v Friends' Provident Life Office* (29 September 2003), the Northern Ireland Court of Appeal said that the statutory provisions were 'designed to prevent an employer from escaping his responsibilities under anti-discrimination legislation by bringing in workers on sub-contract' and that they should 'receive a broad construction which has the effect of providing the statutory protection to a wider range of workers.' The Lord Chief Justice of Northern Ireland added that the purpose of the statutory provisions 'is to ensure that persons who are employed to perform work for someone other than their nominal employers receive the protection of the legislation forbidding discrimination by employers. It is implicit in the philosophy underlying the provision that the principal be in a position to discriminate against the contract worker. The principal must therefore be in a position to influence or control the conditions under which the employee works. It is also inherent in the concept of supplying workers under a contract that it is contemplated by the employer and the principal that the former will provide the services of employees in the course of performance of the contract.'

Contract workers are also employees, by definition, and have a remedy as well if their own employer discriminates against them. This is especially relevant in the case of disability discrimination, where there are special provisions relating to reasonable adjustments by those who employ contract workers.

Barristers and advocates

The Regulations provide that: 'It is unlawful for any person, in relation to the giving, withholding or acceptance of instructions to a barrister, to discriminate against any person by subjecting him to a detriment, or to subject him to harassment.' This makes it unlawful for a solicitor to discriminate in terms of giving instructions against a barrister or pupil on grounds of their sexual orientation, or religion or belief.

The Regulations also make it unlawful for barristers and their clerks to discriminate against, or harass, pupils and tenants (or applicants for pupilages and tenancies).

Similar provision is made in respect of advocates in Scotland.

The Race Relations Act is amended to allow for claims of unlawful discrimination by or against barristers (and advocates in Scotland) to be brought before employment tribunals instead of county courts (or sheriff courts in Scotland) as was previously the case. This will apply where the alleged discrimination is on grounds of race, ethnic or national origin.

The similar change made to the Disability Discrimination Act is discussed in more detail in the strand-specific chapter on disability.

Claims against barristers and advocates will be heard by employment tribunals.

Partnerships

The Religion or Belief and Sexual Orientation Regulations make it unlawful for a firm to discriminate against, or harass, a partner or an applicant for a partnership. The circumstances covered range from the firm's arrangements for determining to whom they should offer a partnership to the circumstances in which a partnership is brought to an end. These provisions are similar to the Race Relations Act 1976, s 10.

The DDA is amended by new s 6A, which has the same effect and also imposes a duty of reasonable adjustment.

Trade organisations

The Religion or Belief and Sexual Orientation Regulations apply to 'trade organisations', which is defined as 'an organisation of workers, an organisation of employers, or any other organisation whose members carry on a particular profession or trade for the purposes of which the organisation exists.' These provisions are similar to the Race Relations Act 1976, s 11.

The Regulations make it unlawful for a trade organisation, such as a trade union, to discriminate against a member or an applicant for membership, or to subject them to harassment. The circumstances covered include refusing to admit the person to membership, affording access to benefits, or depriving the person of membership.

There are similar provisions in the Race Relations and Disability Discrimination Acts.

Qualifications bodies

The Religion or Belief and Sexual Orientation Regulations make it unlawful for a body that confers professional or trade qualifications to discriminate against a person by refusing to confer, or in the terms on which it confers, such a qualification or by withdrawing or varying the terms of a qualification.

Qualifications bodies are also brought within the scope of the DDA for the first time.

'Qualifications body' is defined as 'any authority or body that can confer a professional or trade qualification' other than an institution of further and higher education, or discrimination by a school against its pupils.

'Professional or trade qualification' means 'any authorisation or qualification which is needed for, or facilitates engagement in, a particular profession or trade.'

These provisions are directly parallel to the Race Relations Act 1976, s 12 and in *Patterson v Legal Services Commission* [2003] EWCA Civ 1558, [2004] IRLR 153, CA, the Court of Appeal took a liberal approach to s 12. It ruled that when the Legal Services Commission grants a franchise to a solicitor, it is conferring an authorisation on the franchisee to perform publicly funded legal services for its clients because the franchise 'facilitates' engagement in the profession of solicitor, in that it makes it easier or less difficult to carry on the profession.

Discrimination complaints against qualifications bodies are heard by employment tribunals, except where there is a statutory appeals procedure under which the alleged discriminatory act may be challenged. If there is such a procedure, then that must be used instead.

Vocational training providers

The Religion or Belief and Sexual Orientation Regulations make it unlawful for a 'training provider' that helps fit people for employment to discriminate against, or subject to harassment, a person who is undergoing training or seeking so to do.

'Training' is defined as including 'facilities for training' and 'practical work experience provided by an employer to a person whom he does not employ'. 'Training provider' means 'any person who provides, or makes arrangements for the provision of, training which would help fit another person for any employment', but does not include an employer in

relation to training of its own employees (which is covered under the employment provisions), a school in relation to its pupils or an institution of further and higher education.

These provisions encompass training provided by conference organisations and professional organisations. If a conference organisation refused requests to provide a vegetarian alternative at lunch at a one-day conference on employment law, for example, it could be liable for a claim of indirect discrimination by members of several religious and belief groups.

Employment agencies and career guidance

The Religion or Belief and Sexual Orientation Regulations make it unlawful for an employment agency to discriminate against a person in the terms on which the agency offers to provide any of its services, or by refusing to provide any of its services or in the way it provides any of its services.

An 'employment agency' is defined as 'a person who, for profit or not, provides services for the purpose of finding employment for workers or supplying employers with workers ... .' The definition also extends to 'guidance on careers and any other services related to employment', other than schools and institutions of further and higher education. These provisions are directly parallel to the Race Relations Act 1976, s 14. There are similar provisions in the Disability Discrimination Act 1995.

Institutions of further and higher education

The Religion or Belief and Sexual Orientation Regulations make it unlawful for an institution that provides further or higher education to discriminate against, or harass, a student, or those who have applied to be a student.

The Regulations cover universities, most sixth-form colleges and any other institutions in the further and higher education sectors.

Unlike the other provisions of the Regulations, however, if a student wishes to bring a complaint against an institution of further and higher education, this must be done in a county court in England and Wales, or a sheriff court in Scotland. This is already the case under the comparable provisions in the Race Relations and Disability Discrimination Acts.

Police

The Religion or Belief and Sexual Orientation Regulations ensure that all police constables enjoy the same protection from discrimination and harassment as employees. The DDA (Amendment) Regulations include similar provisions. These parallel the changes made as regards the police by the Race Relations (Amendment) Act 2000.

The holding of the office of police constable is deemed to be treated as 'employment' for the purposes of the Regulations. The chief officer of police is made liable, as if he were the employer, for an act of discrimination or harassment committed by one police officer against another in the course of his or her employment.

Other rights

Constructive dismissal

All of the Regulations make clear that the definition of 'dismissal' includes termination of employment via the employee terminating their own employment 'in circumstances such that he is entitled to terminate it without notice by reason of the conduct of the employer' – ie to treat themselves as having been constructively dismissed.

This resolves uncertainty created by the difference between the definition of dismissal in the discrimination statutes and that in the Employment Rights Act 1996, and conflicting case law under the Race Relations and Disability Discrimination Acts as to whether an employee who resigns in circumstances amounting to a constructive dismissal can bring a claim.

Relationships that have come to an end

A major legal issue under the old discrimination legislation was whether it only applied to acts of

discrimination that occurred during the employment relationship, or whether it extended to acts of discrimination that occurred after the relationship had come to an end.

In June 2003, in *Rhys-Harper v Relaxion Group plc/ D'Souza v London Borough of Lambeth/Jones v 3M Healthcare* [2003] UKHL 33, [2003] IRLR 484, HL, the House of Lords ruled that an employment tribunal has jurisdiction under the Sex Discrimination, Race Relations and Disability Discrimination Acts to consider a complaint of discrimination that relates only to acts that are alleged to have taken place after the complainant's employment has come to an end. However, that decision was largely overtaken by implementation of the new Regulations.

The enforcement provisions of the EU Directives oblige Member States to ensure that judicial procedures are available to all persons who consider themselves wronged by failure to apply the principle of equal treatment to them, 'even after the relationship in which the discrimination is alleged to have occurred has ended.'

The Regulations provide in respect of all the strands that it is unlawful for an employer to discriminate against a former employee, by subjecting them to a detriment or to harassment, where 'the discrimination arises out of and is closely connected to' the employment relationship. The Regulations stipulate:

'(1) In this regulation a "relevant relationship" is a relationship during the course of which an act of discrimination or harassment by one party to the relationship ("A") against the other party to it ("B") would be unlawful by virtue of any provision of this Part.

(2) Where a relevant relationship has come to an end, it is unlawful for A—
(a) to discriminate against B by subjecting him to a detriment; or
(b) to subject B to harassment,
where the discrimination or harassment arises out of and is closely connected to that relationship.'

These provisions were included with all the new Regulations, which means that the changes as regards the Disability Discrimination Act will not come into force until October 2004.

The main issues that are covered by the provisions on relationships that have come to an end are references in respect of former employees and access to facilities that are offered to other ex-employees. The kind of case that will now be caught is the former employer who refuses to provide a reference, or who provides an adverse reference, because of the employee's race or religion or disability or sexual orientation, or because they brought discrimination proceedings against the employer. The ACAS Guide on religion or belief gives the following example: 'A manager is approached by someone from another organisation saying that Mr "Z" has applied for a job and asks for a reference. The manager says that he cannot recommend the worker on the grounds that he did not "fit in" because he refused to socialise in the pub with his colleagues (his religion forbade alcohol). This worker may have been discriminated against on the grounds of his religion after his working relationship with the organisation has ended.'

It is notable that the wording places no time limit on the obligation not to discriminate in this way (although the normal time limit of three months from the alleged act of discrimination itself will apply to bringing claims). The issue is treated entirely as one of causation: that is to say, was the reason the former employee received a bad reference due to the fact that they previously complained that they had been discriminated against? The DTI explanatory notes point out that: 'the further removed the alleged act of discrimination or harassment is from the former working relationship, in both time and context, the less likely it is that a person will be able to establish the necessary close connection to the former relationship. So an incident that takes place a number of years after the relationship has ended, or in a social context unrelated to that relationship, is unlikely to fall under' the Regulations.

An interesting aspect to the new provisions is that they specifically provide that an act of post-employment discrimination taking place after the new Regulations came into force is unlawful even where the relationship came to an end before the relevant Regulations came into force.

The practical implication for employers relates to policies concerning references. The general message coming from data protection interests is that records relating to employees should not be kept very long. Some employers only retain personnel records in respect of former employees for several months. The risk is that if no reference is provided to an ex-employee who has previously brought a grievance complaining of discrimination, or if an adverse reference is provided such as by suggesting that they were a troublemaker, a claim of post-employment discrimination may result.

Positive action

The Religion or Belief and Sexual Orientation Regulations allow employers to take positive action to encourage persons of a particular religion or belief, or sexual orientation, to take advantage of opportunities for doing particular work or by affording them access to training facilities for such work.

Such positive action is permitted 'where it reasonably appears to the person doing the act that it prevents or compensates for disadvantages linked to' sexual orientation, or religion or belief, as the case may be, 'suffered by persons of that sexual orientation' etc doing that work or likely to take up that work. This would cover the fact that persons of that group have been discriminated against in the past in gaining access to the particular job and are therefore under-represented.

By allowing positive action where the employer believes that the measure to be taken compensates for disadvantages, the Religion and Sexual Orientation Regulations go somewhat further than the Race Relations Act in this respect. The latter allows positive action only where it reasonably appears to the employer that 'the proportion of persons of that [racial] group among those doing that work in Great Britain was small in comparison with the proportion of persons of that group among the population of Great Britain.' Since it would be practically impossible for an employer to document the proportion of gay men, for example, doing particular work compared with their proportion in the population as a whole, the more liberal test is common sense.

As with the other prohibited grounds, positive action is permitted to the extent that relevant vocational training can be restricted to members of the group and they can be encouraged to apply for particular jobs. However, positive discrimination at the point of selection in favour of members of an under-represented group is unlawful, in that it would amount to direct discrimination against members of other groups.

The DTI explanatory notes give the following illustration: 'if a factory owner has a small number of Hindu employees despite being based in an area with a large Hindu population, when advertising for new recruits he could include a statement that "applications from Hindus are particularly welcome". However, it would be unlawful … to give preference to a Hindu job applicant over an applicant of another faith simply because the employer wishes to have more Hindu employees.'

The ACAS Guide on religion or belief guide adds that employers may wish to consider positive measures such as 'training their existing employees for work that has historically been the preserve of individuals from a particular religion or belief' and 'advertisements which encourage applications from a minority religion but making it clear that selection will be on merit without reference to religion or belief.'

There are parallel provisions relating to trade organisations, including trade unions, allowing them to encourage those from disadvantaged groups to become members.

Chapter 6

Employer liability and enforcement

Employer liability

The Religion or Belief and Sexual Orientation Regulations embody the same principles, using identical language, in respect of liability for discrimination as is already found in the Race Relations and Disability Discrimination Acts.

There are three key general principles: (1) an employer is legally liable for discriminatory or harassive acts of its employees whether or not the employer knows about them; (2) an employer has a defence to liability if it has taken reasonably practicable steps to prevent the employee from doing the unlawful act; (3) an employee can be personally liable for proven discrimination or harassment.

Legal liability

Like the other discrimination statutes, the new Regulations provide that 'anything done by a person in the course of his employment shall be treated for the purposes of these Regulations as done by his employer as well as by him, whether or not it was done with the employer's knowledge or approval.'

Ever since the decision of the Court of Appeal in *Jones v Tower Boot Co Ltd* [1997] IRLR 168, the words 'in the course of employment' have been given a broad and purposive construction, especially in the context of racial and sexual harassment, with the aim of encouraging employers to take preventative steps to help ensure that discrimination does not take place.

As Waite LJ put it in *Tower Boot*, the policy of s 32 – the employer liability provision in the Race Relations Act 1976, and its counterpart in sex discrimination law, 'is to deter racial and sexual harassment in the workplace through a widening of the net of responsibility beyond the guilty employees themselves, by making all employers additionally liable for such harassment, and then supplying them with the reasonable steps defence under s 32(3), which will exonerate the conscientious employer who has used his best endeavours to prevent such harassment, and will encourage all employers who have not yet undertaken such endeavours to take the steps necessary to make the same defence available in their own workplace.'

In this context, employers need to bear in mind that this broad interpretation of the concept of the 'course of employment' has been held to extend to discrimination, and especially harassment, which takes place at work-related events outside the workplace. In *Chief Constable of the Lincolnshire Police v Stubbs* [1999] IRLR 81, for example, the EAT upheld a finding that a police officer was acting in the 'course of his employment' within the meaning of the Sex Discrimination Act when he subjected the applicant to inappropriate sexual behaviour, even though the incidents occurred at social events away from the police station. According to Morison J, when there is a social gathering of work colleagues, it is entirely appropriate for the tribunal to consider whether or not the circumstances show that what was occurring was an extension of their employment.

Employer's defence

An employer has a statutory defence to acts of discrimination or harassment by its employees if it can prove that it 'took such steps as were reasonably practicable to prevent the employee from doing' the relevant act.

The DTI explanatory notes suggest that an example of potential defences for a harassment claim might be where an employer 'can show that he has an equal opportunities policy and carries out training to ensure that all employees know that such behaviour is not permitted, and/or that he has

disciplined employees in the past who have been guilty of such harassment.'

In a recent Court of Appeal case considering this issue, *Croft v Royal Mail Group plc* [2003] EWCA Civ 1045, [2003] IRLR 592, CA, it was held that in considering whether an action that it is submitted the employers should have taken is reasonably practicable, it is permissible to take into account the extent of the difference, if any, which the action is likely to make. According to the Court of Appeal, the concept of reasonable practicability entitles the employer in this context to consider whether the time, effort and expense of the suggested measures are disproportionate to the result likely to be achieved.

Aiding unlawful acts

The Religion or Belief and Sexual Orientation Regulations provide that 'a person who knowingly aids another person to do an act made unlawful by these Regulations shall be treated for the purpose of these Regulations as himself doing an unlawful act.' They then go on to specify that, for this purpose, 'an employee ... for whose act the employer or principal is liable' under the employer liability provisions, or would be so liable but for the employer's defence to liability, 'shall be deemed to aid the doing of the act by the employer'. Thus, the combined effect of the two sections on legal liability is that the person doing the act, as well as their employer, acts unlawfully. The same language is found in the Race Relations and Disability Discrimination Acts.

The meaning of the wording in the Race Relations Act was considered by the Court of Appeal in *Yeboah v Crofton* [2002] EWCA Civ 794, [2002] IRLR 634, CA, where it was confirmed that even if an employer is not legally liable because it was able to show that it took such steps as were reasonably practicable to prevent the employee from doing the act in question, an employee can be personally liable for 'knowingly' aiding the unlawful act of the employer.

As a result, it will often be the case, especially in harassment complaints, that an applicant will be advised to name as respondents both the individual harasser and the employer, since the individual harasser would remain legally liable even if the employer was able to rely on the defence that it had taken reasonably practicable steps to prevent the act.

Enforcement

Complaints of discrimination or harassment by employers and most other complaints of discrimination under the new Regulations will be heard by employment tribunals. The statutory provisions here are the same as for complaints under the Race Relations and Disability Discrimination Acts.

There is no change to the existing law under the Race Relations Act and Disability Discrimination Act on the remedies available for successful complainants, and the same remedies will be available under the Religion or Belief and Sexual Orientation Regulations. The tribunal may make a declaration, including an action recommendation: 'a recommendation that the respondent take within a specified period action appearing to the tribunal to be practicable for the purpose of obviating or reducing the adverse effect on the complainant of any act of discrimination to which the complaint relates.' A typical recommendation that is made under these provisions is that the employers ensure that the individual responsible for the discrimination is given awareness training within a specified period.

There is no limit on compensation that may be awarded, which can include damages for injury to feelings.

Questionnaire procedure

All the Regulations provide for a questionnaire procedure whereby an aggrieved person can question the employer in cases of alleged discrimination. Such a procedure previously existed under the Race Relations Act and the Disability Discrimination Act. However, previously, there was

no stipulated time limit within which the respondent to a questionnaire had to reply. The statutes merely provided that if the reply was not within a 'reasonable period', the court or tribunal could draw adverse inferences from the respondent's lack of response.

The new provisions establish an eight-week time limit from the time a questionnaire is served for a respondent to reply to questions about alleged acts of discrimination or harassment. According to the Home Office, the provision 'provides clarity by not leaving it to the courts to decide what is a "reasonable period" within which respondents have to reply. Another benefit is that cases will now progress and be resolved more quickly.'

If the respondent fails to reply, or if the reply is evasive or equivocal, the tribunal or court may draw adverse inferences, 'including an inference that he committed an unlawful act', that discrimination took place.

Suggested forms for questions and replies are set out in Schedules to the Regulations. There is no requirement, however, on an applicant or a respondent to use the forms set out in the Schedules.

Time limits

The usual three-month time limit from the alleged act of discrimination applies for presenting an employment tribunal complaint under the Religion or Belief and Sexual Orientation Regulations.

All the time limits for presenting a complaint may be changed in accordance with powers taken by the Secretary of State under the Employment Act 2002. This envisages the mandatory use of statutory grievance procedures, in most circumstances, before a complaint to an employment tribunal will be permitted (although harassment complaints are likely to be excluded from this requirement). Regulations implementing these provisions are expected to come into force in October 2004 and are likely to apply to all the discrimination jurisdictions.

Strand-specific issues

Race discrimination

The Race Relations Act 1976 (Amendment) Regulations 2003 implement the EU Race Discrimination Directive 2000/43. The Regulations came into force on 19 July 2003. The main changes of practical significance are those that affect all the different strands of discrimination covered by the new Regulations, including a new definition of indirect discrimination, a freestanding definition of racial harassment, provision for unlawful acts after a relationship has ended and changes to the burden of proof. These were discussed the first part of this book.

These changes are of considerable importance, but they only will affect some forms of race discrimination under the Race Relations Act and not others. This is because of the mismatch in the definitions of prohibited grounds of discrimination as between the new Regulations and the Race Relations Act.

Colour and nationality not covered

The Race Relations Act prohibits discrimination on grounds of 'race', 'colour', 'ethnic or national origin', or 'nationality' (defined by the Act as including 'citizenship'). However, the EU Race Discrimination Directive covers only discrimination on grounds of 'race', 'ethnic or national origin' but not 'colour' or 'nationality'.

It is not entirely clear how 'colour' will be interpreted, now that a distinction has been drawn between 'colour' and 'race'. The Commission for Racial Equality has pointed out that it is particularly 'illogical to implement the principle of equal treatment by providing for greater protection from discrimination on grounds or race and ethnic or national origin but not colour. The principal trigger for racially discriminatory behaviour is frequently colour: discriminators will seldom know the victim's ethnic or national origin and sometimes not the racial group but "colour" is a visibly different characteristic.'

Since the origins of race discrimination legislation lie in the decision by Parliament to make operating a 'colour bar' unlawful, it would be regrettable if a lower legal standard operated as regards discrimination on grounds of 'colour' than in respect of other forms of race discrimination. It is at least arguable, however, that 'colour' in practice is subsumed in 'race', and that accordingly any discrimination on grounds of 'colour' would fall within the new definitions.

That is not the case, however, with 'nationality'. 'Nationality' is distinct from 'national origin'. It refers mainly to 'nationality' in the legal sense, and thus to citizenship. It clearly was not the intention of the Directive to cover discrimination based on nationality. In UK law, 'nationality' has been defined rather widely. In *BBC Scotland v Souster* [2001] IRLR 150, the Inner House of the Court of Session in Scotland ruled that 'nationality' is not defined exclusively by reference to citizenship. Nationality can encompass a change in nationality, and can be referable to present nationality. In that case, it was held that an applicant could be discriminated against on grounds of his English 'nationality' where that nationality was acquired by adherence or adoption since his birth or because he was perceived to have become a member of the racial group, the English.

Because the Government decided to implement the new discrimination Directives by Regulations made under the European Communities Act 1972, s 2 this meant that the Race Relations (Amendment) Regulations could not, and do not, cover race discrimination complaints brought on grounds of colour or nationality. As a result, the new definitions of indirect discrimination and harassment, the shift in the burden of proof, the new provisions relating to the genuine occupational requirement exception, the new test for employment in Great Britain and other changes made by the 2003 Regulations apply only to discrimination on the ground of race, ethnic or national origin, and not to discrimination on grounds of colour or nationality, in respect of which the previous provisions of the Race Relations Act are unaltered.

The result is that there are now two definitions of indirect discrimination that differ according to whether what is challenged relates to the impact of a practice on a person's racial group as defined by their race or ethnic or national origins on the one hand, or their nationality on the other hand. In the latter case, the old definition, necessitating proof of a 'requirement or condition' and with the old justification defence, continues to apply. The new definitions will only apply to cases of race, ethnic or national origin discrimination. This means that a 'provision, criterion or practice' can now be challenged if it has an adverse impact on a group defined by race, ethnic or national origins, and that the new defence of whether the employer can show that that is a 'proportionate means of achieving a legitimate aim' will apply.

Similarly, in a case of direct discrimination, the new burden of proof provisions will apply to cases of alleged race, ethnic or national origin discrimination, but not to cases of nationality discrimination, where the less stringent standard set out in *King v Great Britain-China Centre* continues to apply.

Furthermore, the new freestanding definition of harassment will apply only to race, ethnic or national origin harassment, but not to harassment based on nationality or colour, which will continue to be judged in accordance with the previous statutory language. Thus, a very different standard will apply for an applicant attempting to prove unlawful harassment on nationality grounds than on grounds of race, ethnic or national origin.

This may well present real practical problems. Which legal standards will apply when a tribunal hears a claim under the Race Relations Act from a woman from Turkey who has been turned down for a promotion? In many cases, applicants claiming race discrimination will not be in a position to say whether the ground for their treatment was their 'national origin' rather than their 'nationality', and will be advised to tick both boxes on the originating application. Whether the applicant's nationality or her national origin (or both) played any part in the decision will only emerge after all the evidence is heard and tribunals will have to operate on the assumption that either, neither or both could be the case.

The Government's 2002 consultative document *Equality and Diversity: The Way Ahead* promised: 'We intend to rectify any inconsistencies that occur in the amended Race Relations Act as a result when an opportunity arises.' It is to be hoped that the opportunity will soon arise.

Indirect discrimination

The new definition of indirect discrimination discussed earlier in this book means that the old limitation that policies could only be challenged if they took the form of a 'requirement or condition' will no longer apply.

The CRE gives as examples of provisions, criteria or practices that might be indirectly discriminatory: 'a firm's policy of filling senior management positions internally, from a pool of senior and middle managers, most of whom are white' and 'a word-of-mouth recruitment policy in a firm where the majority of the workforce are Asian'.

The new definition, as we have noted, will make proof of indirect discrimination easier in that statistical comparisons of the impact of a requirement on different racial groups will no longer be required. As the CRE points out, 'statistical data demonstrating the difficulty a group has in complying may be hard to come by, and, although it is not vital, its absence can make it difficult to prove a differential impact.'

Racial harassment: are the Regulations regressive?

The new freestanding definition of harassment, the Race Relations Act 1976, s 3A (added by the Race Relations Regulations), provides:

'(1) A person ("A") subjects another to harassment ... where, on grounds of race or ethnic or national origins, he engages in unwanted conduct which has the purpose or effect of –

(a) violating that other person's dignity, or
(b) creating an intimidating, hostile, degrading, humiliating or offensive environment for him.'

(2) Conduct shall be regarded as having the effect specified in para (a) or (b) of subsection (1) only if, having regard to all the circumstances, including in particular the perception of that other person, it should reasonably be considered as having that effect.'

As discussed in the chapter on harassment, the controversial question is the scope of sub-s (2) and, in particular, what circumstances other than that of the perception of the complainant are to be regarded as relevant to whether unwanted conduct had the effect of violating that person's dignity or creating an intimidating, hostile, degrading, humiliating or offensive environment?

So far as race discrimination is concerned, the most likely factual scenario is that of racial banter and abuse. For example, a black applicant claims that the behaviour of one of her colleagues in using racially offensive terms to her, or in her presence, has violated her dignity or created a hostile working environment for her. The harasser admits using the words in question but says that he was only joking and did not mean to be offensive.

The key issue is whether the tribunal can take this absence of a discriminatory motive into account, as one of the circumstances, in whether the conduct should reasonably be considered as violating the claimant's dignity or creating a hostile working environment.

In the explanatory note to the Race Relations (Amendment) Regulations, the Home Office says: 'Subsection (2) of the new section stipulates that unwanted conduct has the effect indicated above where it should reasonably be considered as having that effect, taking into account the views of the person claiming to have been harassed and the motives of the alleged perpetrator.'

This is both legally problematic and misguided from a policy standpoint. One can see how a tribunal can take an objective view as to whether particular conduct could 'reasonably' be considered as racially offensive. That involves an evaluation of the behaviour concerned, from the reasonable standpoint of the person experiencing it. If a reasonable person in that position would not be offended by the behaviour, then it should not be regarded as harassive. The law does not protect 'over-sensitive' complainants. This assessment is from the perspective of the recipient. It should not entail the tribunal deciding how they themselves would regard the behaviour.

It is not at all clear, however, how the motive of the harasser is a relevant ingredient in the assessment of whether unwanted conduct had the effect of violating a person's dignity, or creating an intimidating, hostile, degrading, humiliating or offensive environment. That it emerges that the harasser did not mean to be offensive does not in any way reduce the harm caused to the recipient of the offensive behaviour.

This proposition is reinforced by the language of the Regulation itself. It distinguishes between harassment having the 'purpose' of violating dignity or creating an offensive environment, and harassment that has that 'effect'. Subsection (2) relates only to harassment that does not have such a purpose. There is no meaningful distinction apparent here between 'purpose' and 'motive'. Therefore, sub-s (2) is, by definition, confined to cases where the harasser did not have a discriminatory motive. Accordingly, it would be inappropriate to further take that into account in construing sub-s (2).

It is also strongly arguable that contrary to the Home Office advice, an interpretation of s 3A2(2) that allows a lack of a discriminatory motive to be a defence would be regressive and contrary to the Race Discrimination Directive, Article 6(2) of which provides:

> 'The implementation of this Directive shall under no circumstances constitute grounds for a reduction in the level of protection against discrimination already afforded by Member States in the fields covered by this Directive.'

Prior to the new Regulations coming into force, a racial harassment complainant merely had to establish that they were subjected to a 'detriment'. Regulation 5(2) amends the definitions section in the Race Relations Act 1976, s 78 by providing that '"detriment" does not include conduct of a nature such as to constitute harassment under s 3A.' Thus, someone experiencing racial abuse will not be able to argue that they have been subjected to an unlawful detriment, but will now have to establish that their case satisfies the ingredients of the definition of harassment. For the reasons given above, it is strongly arguable that this means that it will be more difficult for some applicants subjected to racial abuse to establish a case of unlawful discrimination than it was under the previous law.

Finally, there is the additional potential problem in a racial harassment case of mixed grounds with different legal standards, or of deciding which is the correct legal standard. If a woman from Nigeria complains that a colleague at work makes remarks that 'all you Nigerian women are crooks', is this a claim of harassment on grounds of national origin, in which case the new test in the Regulations of racial harassment will apply? Or is it a claim of harassment on grounds of nationality, in which case it will have to be determined whether the conduct was detrimental treatment in accordance with the statutory principles, as interpreted, before the Regulations came into force?

Genuine occupational requirements

The Race Relations Act previously had a specific list of narrowly-drawn 'genuine occupational qualifications', which applied where the job involved being in a dramatic performance, being an artist's model, working in a place where food or drink was served, or providing persons of a racial group with personal services.

These have been replaced, where the alleged grounds of discrimination are race or ethnic or national origins, by the concept of 'genuine occupational requirements' (GOR). The Act as amended allows an employer to restrict a job to people of a particular race, ethnic or national origin, if that meets the test of being a genuine occupational requirement for the job.

The new statutory language, found in s 4A(2) states:

> 'This subsection applies only where, having regard to the nature of the employment or the context in which it is carried out –
>
> (a) being of a particular race or particular ethnic or national origins is a genuine and determining occupational requirement, and
>
> (b) it is proportionate to apply that requirement in the particular case; and
>
> (c) either –
>   (i) the person to whom the requirement is applied does not meet it, or
>   (ii) the employer is not satisfied, and in all the circumstances it is reasonable for him not to be satisfied, that that person meets it.'

Note that in order to satisfy this exception, being of a particular race etc must not only be a genuine occupational requirement for a particular post, it must also be a 'determining' requirement for that post – ie it must decisive. Even then, it must also be proportionate to apply the requirement. However, the new definition of a genuine occupational requirement can be applied not just where the nature of the job calls for an employee from a particular racial group but also where the context in which it is carried out demands it.

As with the new genuine occupational requirements relating to religion and sexual orientation, s 4A(2)(c) allows an employer to establish a GOR exception on the basis of a reasonable perception about a person's ability to meet a particular requirement. Section 4A(1)(c) allows a GOR to operate in respect of a dismissal. This is not possible under the existing exceptions for genuine occupational qualifications in the Race Relations Act 1976, s 5 and thus is also arguably regressive.

If a genuine occupational requirement operates, the employer will be able to lawfully discriminate on grounds of race or ethnic or national origin in recruitment, promotion or transfer to a job, dismissal

from a post and in training for a job. The CRE gives as an example of the difference the new provisions will make that of an Asian women's refuge that wants an Asian woman for the post of staff manager. The CRE points out that 'previously, it would not have been possible to rely on the equivalent exemption under the Race Relations Act for such posts … . This is no longer the case, but the employer has to show that: the nature of the job or the context in which it is carried out requires the manager to be Asian; and the benefits of employing an Asian manager outweigh the effects of discriminating against other racial groups.'

It is arguable that the broader definition of a genuine occupational requirement is regressive, both to the extent that it allows a defence to be raised generally in circumstances that did not fall within the previous limited genuine occupational qualification exceptions and, more particularly, because it allows an employer a potential defence based on a perceived inability to comply with a GOR regardless of whether the GOR was, in fact, satisfied. Suppose an employer considered that it required someone of Afro-Caribbean origin for a particular welfare post, and it rejected a candidate because he did not appear to be racially Afro-Caribbean in that he had a pale skin colour. Leaving to one side the question whether this is discrimination on grounds of colour (and thus not covered by the new GOR anyway, or discrimination on grounds of race), it would not have been possible for such an erroneous, though reasonable view, to found a GOR under the former legislation.

Private households

Employment 'for the purposes of a private household' was previously excluded from the provisions of the Race Relations Act. The Race Discrimination Directive, however, requires Member States to abolish any laws contrary to the principle of equal treatment. As a result this exclusion has been removed, but only insofar as it relates to the relevant grounds covered by the 2003 Regulations.

The Home Office guidance proudly says: 'discrimination in employment in a private household (for example, employment as a nanny, cleaner, or gardener), on the relevant grounds, will no longer be allowed. This will enhance the rights of the people who work in these fields.' This is true but because the 'relevant grounds' are restricted, it means that it is now unlawful to discriminate on grounds of race or ethnic or national origins as regards employment for the purposes of a private household, but it remains lawful to so discriminate if the grounds for discriminating are the person's nationality or colour.

Employers who regard it as genuinely necessary for a person to be of a particular race or of a particular ethnic or national origin in order to carry out particular employment in a private household will have to try to rely on the provisions relating to genuine occupational requirements.

Other areas in which scope has been widened

Article 14 of the Race Discrimination Directive requires Member States to 'take necessary measures to ensure that any laws, regulations and administrative provisions contrary to the principle of equal treatment are abolished'. In order to comply with this requirement, a number of exemptions in the Race Relations Act were removed, at least partially.

These include:
- *Training for those not ordinarily resident in Great Britain.* British employers have been allowed to discriminate on racial grounds when employing people who come to Great Britain to learn new skills and then return to their own country or elsewhere to use those skills. The Regulations remove this ability to discriminate in so far as it relates to discrimination on grounds of race, ethnic or national origin. It will still be possible, however, to provide these skills to someone on the basis of their nationality or colour.
- *Charities as employers.* Previously, charities were not subject to the employment provisions of

the Race Relations Act 1976. Charities that targeted their benefits at particular racial groups were able to recruit staff from a particular racial group. Charities are now subject to the employment provisions in the Act in the same way as other employers, so far as concerns discrimination or harassment on grounds of race, ethnic or national origin. Charities will be able to rely on genuine occupational requirements when recruiting staff to undertake certain roles where the nature of the employment requires someone of a particular race or of a particular ethnic or national origin. Charities will continue to be able to rely on the existing exemption for the purpose of recruiting staff who need to be of a particular nationality, as the ground of nationality is excluded from the scope of the Directive.
- *Seamen recruited abroad.* The Race Relations Act formerly provided an exemption in respect of the employment of seafarers. Employers are no longer allowed to discriminate on the grounds of race, ethnic or national origins in relation to the employment of seafarers recruited overseas. Discrimination on grounds of nationality continues to be exempted from the Race Relations Act, but only in relation to remuneration, and not to treatment and conditions on board.
- *Partnerships.* The Race Relations Act formerly provided that partnerships of fewer than six persons were exempt from its provisions. The Regulations removed this exemption in relation to discrimination on grounds of race, ethnic or national origin, so that partnerships of any size are subject to the same rules under the Race Relations Act in relation to discrimination on those grounds. This means that it is unlawful for any partnership to discriminate against or subject to harassment on grounds of race, ethnic or national origin a partner or person who has applied for a partnership. Discrimination on grounds of colour or nationality by partnerships of six or less continues to be excluded from the scope of the Act.

Chapter 8

Discrimination on grounds of religion or belief

The Employment Equality (Religion or Belief) Regulations 2003 bring within the scope of discrimination law for the first time Muslims, Hindus and a wide range of other religious and belief groups. Until now, there has been no remedy against being discriminated on grounds of membership of such groups unless the individuals concerned were also members of a particular racial or ethnic group so as to be able to bring a claim under the Race Relations Act.

The Regulations are important for combating some serious problems of discrimination at work in 21st century Britain against minorities. However, they also present some difficult problems of legal interpretation and of balancing the rights of the religious against those of the non-believer.

The general structure of the Regulations is directly parallel to the Race Relations Act, as it now is after the amendments made by the Race Relations Act (Amendment) Regulations (see Chapter 7). Direct and indirect discrimination in employment on grounds of religion or belief, by way of victimisation or by way of harassment is prohibited. The Regulations extend to discrimination against contract workers and by trade organisations, including trade unions, and by qualifying bodies. Employers are made legally liable for discrimination by their employees and enforcement proceedings can be brought in an employment tribunal.

As mentioned, until now the main route for an employee who wished to complain about direct or indirect discrimination on grounds of religion was the Race Relations Act. In *Mandla v Dowell Lee* [1983] IRLR 209, the House of Lords set out a test for determining what is an 'ethnic group' for the purposes of the Race Relations Act that had the effect of encompassing Sikhs and Jewish people. Applying this test, however, other religious groups, such as Muslims, Rastafarians and Jehovah's Witnesses, were held not to fall within the definition of racial or ethnic group. Muslims, who come from many parts of the world, were unprotected unless the group wishing to complain happened to come from the same country, as in *J H Walker Ltd v Hussain* [1996] IRLR 11, where the employer's refusal to allow Muslim employees time off to celebrate Eid was held to be indirect racial discrimination against Pakistani employees who were disproportionately adversely affected.

Meaning of 'religion or belief'

The EU Framework Employment Directive requires Member States to prohibit discrimination on grounds of 'religion or belief'. However, it contains no definition of 'religion' or 'belief'. The Government resisted calls to provide a detailed definition or set out an exhaustive list of groups that should be regarded as religions. The Regulations merely specify that 'religion or belief' means: 'any religion, religious belief, or similar philosophical belief.'

The use of the term 'any religion' in the definition is deliberately wide, and in line with the broad concept of freedom of religion guaranteed by Article 9 of the European Convention on Human Rights.

The definition certainly covers widely-recognised religions, as well as branches of such religions. The ACAS Guide for employers and employees, *Religion or Belief and the Workplace*, mentions the following as 'commonly practised religions and beliefs' in Britain:

- Baha'i
- Buddhism
- Christianity
- Hinduism
- Islam (Muslims)
- Jainism
- Judaism (Jews)
- Other ancient religions, including Druidry, Paganism and Wicca
- Rastafarianism
- Sikhism
- Zoroastrians.

Because it is drawn without qualification, the definition of 'religion or belief' is also likely to cover fringe religions and, perhaps, membership of cults. The European Court of Human Rights has recognised the Church of Scientology, Krishna Consciousness and the Divine Light Zentrum as religions, for example. Members of such groups will have rights not to be directly or indirectly discriminated against or harassed on grounds of their religion. Whether the definition will cover newer groups such as Raelians, or even Jedi Knights (as revealed during the 2001 census), will only be determined if members of such groups bring complaints of discrimination.

Does 'religious belief' include manifestations of religion?

'Religious belief' must mean something more than membership of a particular religion, since the definition refers both to 'religion' and 'religious belief'.

On the ordinary meaning of the words, a right not to be discriminated against on grounds of one's religious beliefs suggests protection against being discriminated against because of holding a particular view that is part of the religion. For example, if you are a devout Roman Catholic, it is likely to be an important part of your belief system that abortion is unacceptable.

But does the right go further and encompass showing your belief as well? The DTI's explanatory notes acknowledge that 'religious belief' includes adherence to the religion's 'central articles of faith'. However, the DTI draws a sharp distinction between this and manifesting a religious belief. The explanatory notes then say: 'The definition of "religion or belief" does not include the "manifestation" of, or conduct based on or expression of a religion or belief (see also the distinction made in Article 9 ECHR). For example, a person may wear certain clothing, or pray at certain times in accordance with the tenets of her religion, or she may express views, and say or do other things reflecting her beliefs. In such a case it would not in itself constitute direct discrimination on grounds of religion or belief under the Regulations … if a person suffers a disadvantage because she has done or said something in this way. It would only be direct discrimination if a person with different beliefs (or no beliefs) was treated more favourably in similar circumstances. However, if an employer does set down requirements about (for example) clothing or breaks for prayers, these may constitute indirect discrimination … under the Regulations unless they are justified.'

If an employer treats someone unfavourably because they manifest their religious belief, is that necessarily direct discrimination? Or is it only direct discrimination if it can be shown that someone of a different religion is (or would be) treated more favourably? If an employer bans Muslim women from wearing a hijab and Jewish men from wearing a yarmulke, is that religious discrimination against both the Muslim and the Jew, or is it no religious discrimination at all?

This is a very important issue for the way in which the Regulations are interpreted. As we will see, the same interpretation is given by the DTI to the Sexual Orientation Regulations. If discrimination on grounds of expressing a religious belief is direct discrimination without more, it is not capable of being justified by the employer. But if it is not necessarily direct discrimination to treat someone unfavourably because they wear clothing dictated by their religious beliefs or express views reflecting a central tenet of their beliefs, then the right to be discriminated against is quite narrow.

The DTI notes refer to the 'distinction' made by Article 9 of the European Convention on Human Rights. But the definition in Article 9 could be regarded as undermining the DTI's argument. Article 9 says that 'everyone has the right to freedom of … religion … this right includes freedom … to manifest his religion … .' In other words, Article 9 does not say there is a right to freedom of religion and a further additional right to manifest religion. It says that freedom of religion 'includes' freedom to manifest religion. That means that the right encompasses both the right to hold beliefs and the right to manifest those beliefs. This is not surprising: a right to hold beliefs has little meaning if those beliefs cannot be manifested.

It is clear that the right provided by the Convention encompasses both the right to hold beliefs and the right to manifest those beliefs. Interference with the right to manifest beliefs is prima facie a breach of the Convention. It is treated by human rights law as a direct, rather than an indirect, discrimination issue (although it is a qualified right).

In *Kokkinakis v Greece* (1994) 17 EHRR 397, the ECHR held that religious freedom 'implies ... freedom to manifest one's religion. Bearing witness in words and deeds is bound up with the existence of religious convictions.' It also pointed out that the freedom to manifest religion includes the 'right to try to convince one's neighbour', ie proselytising.

The European Court of Justice has consistently held that EU legislation must be interpreted having regard to the European Convention and its interpretation by the Strasbourg Court (see, most recently, *KB v National Health Service Pensions Agency* [2004] IRLR 240. Similarly, British tribunals and courts are under a duty, in accordance with the Human Rights Act, to interpret domestic law, including the new discrimination Regulations in a manner compatible with the Convention Rights guaranteed by the Human Rights Act 1998 (see, most recently, *Pay v Lancashire Probation Service* [2004] IRLR 129). That would tend to suggest that a disadvantage that results from manifesting a religious belief should be regarded as direct discrimination.

On the other hand, there is a very powerful practical attraction in distinguishing between religious beliefs and their manifestation. It would mean that so long as members of a particular religion were not singled out, many of the most controversial issues relating to religious discrimination would be treated as indirect discrimination issues, and capable of justification by the employer. For example, we know that there are many fundamentalist religions that regard homosexuality as an abomination. If a fundamentalist employee tells a gay colleague that they will 'burn in hell' because of their sexual practices, and they complain of harassment, what is the analysis if the employer disciplines the fundamentalist? If they are able to claim that being disciplined necessarily amounted to direct religious discrimination, that would create great practical problems and we know that tribunals will strive to avoid such an outcome.

The DTI explanatory notes actually use this example and arrive at the following conclusion: 'The disciplinary action would not be direct discrimination on grounds of religion or belief if the basis for the treatment of the employee is the statements he has made, not his beliefs themselves. In other words, the

employer could show that he would discipline employees of other faiths (or no faith) in the same way if they made similar statements'.

In our view, this is the right legal analysis: the homophobic employee is not being disciplined for manifesting their religious beliefs as such but instead because they have contravened the employer's policy relating to offensive remarks at work. On that analysis, there is no direct religious discrimination either. But, with respect to the DTI's lawyers, they appear to put forward two theories without recognising the difference between them. The reason why the example works is not because disciplinary action for manifesting a religious belief is not direct discrimination, but instead is because the ground for the treatment was not expressing the religious belief but instead was the contravention of the harassment policy. The employee is being disciplined for their anti-gay statements. They would not be disciplined for quoting the Bible in other contexts.

The rather lengthy discussion of this one issue shows the complexity of these Regulations and how much will depend on how they are interpreted by the tribunals and courts. We return to this point below in discussing direct discrimination.

Similar philosophical belief

The Regulations also cover discrimination against someone on grounds of a 'similar philosophical belief' to 'religion' or 'belief'. Note that the word 'similar' is not used in the Framework Employment Directive, which requires Member States to make it unlawful to discriminate on grounds of 'religion or belief'.

The DTI explanatory notes say that the phrase 'similar philosophical belief' 'does not include any philosophical or political belief unless it is similar to a religious belief.' They explain: 'That does not mean that a belief must include faith in a God/Gods or worship of a God/Gods to be "similar" to a religious belief. It means that the belief in question should be a profound belief affecting a person's way of life or perception of the world. Effectively, the belief should occupy a place in the person's life parallel to that filled by the God/Gods of those holding a particular religious belief.'

This accords with the interpretation of Article 9 by the European Court of Human Rights. In *Campbell and Cosans v United Kingdom* (1982) 4 EHRR 293, the Court said that: 'The term "beliefs" ... denotes a certain level of cogency, seriousness, cohesion and importance.'

According to the DTI, examples of beliefs that would fall within the Regulations are 'atheism' and 'humanism'; 'examples of beliefs which generally do not are support for a political party, support for a football team.'

Most of us would agree that support for Manchester United cannot rightly be regarded as a 'philosophical belief', but what about support for a political party or other political causes? In *McFeeley v United Kingdom* (1980) 3 EHRR 161, the ECHR said that 'belief' means 'more than just mere opinions or deeply held feelings; there must be a holding of spiritual or philosophical convictions that have an identifiable formal content.'

It is clear that the Religion or Belief Regulations are not intended to provide protection against discrimination on grounds of 'political opinion', in contrast to the position in Northern Ireland, where 'political opinion' is protected by the Fair Employment and Treatment (Northern Ireland) Order. They are unlikely to protect an employee from being discriminated against on grounds of membership of the Labour or Conservative Party, for example. Nor are they likely to cover political or ideological beliefs such as in the legalisation of drugs or opposition to road building.

Some political beliefs, however, may be similar to religious beliefs, at least in the way that they are practised by particular individuals. Pacifism, for example, might be said to involve 'a profound belief affecting a person's way of life or perception of the world'. It was accepted as a belief for the purposes of Article 9 of the European Convention in *Arrowsmith v United Kingdom* (1980) 19 DR 5. An employee who was harassed for opposing the war against Iraq because of his or her pacifist beliefs, for example, might be able to bring a claim that they were discriminated against on grounds of their belief.

Membership of the British National Party might be said to involve philosophical beliefs about the position of different races, nationalities and religions. An employer who dismissed a BNP activist who expressed his or her views in the workplace offending other employees is unlikely to be found to have discriminated (because, as discussed above, the grounds for dismissal presumably would be a contravention of the employer's policy), but the position might be less clear cut if the employee was dismissed merely because other employees found membership of the BNP objectionable, or if the employee was dismissed for political activities outside the workplace. (Such a case would also raise issues as to the right to freedom of expression under Article 10).

What about animal rights activists or vegans? There are a number of religious groups that do not permit eating meat, so an employer who refuses a request to provide vegetarian alternatives in the canteen is now risking a claim of religious discrimination.

Equally, some religious beliefs may include political beliefs. The Wahhabi strand of Islam practised in Saudi Arabia or Roman Catholic liberation theology as practised in Latin America are just two examples. Closer to home, in *R (Williamson) v Secretary of State for Education and Employment* [2002] EWCA Civ 1820, [2003] QB 1300, CA, a majority of the Court of Appeal held that the claimants' belief in the use of mild corporal punishment as part of a Christian education was a 'belief' for the purposes of Article 9 of the Convention.

It is difficult to see how the Regulations can disentangle the political opinions held as part of those religious beliefs from the religious belief itself, anymore than it would be appropriate to separate one part of a religion's theology from another.

Absence of belief and discrimination in favour of co-religionists

The definition in the Regulations prohibits discrimination 'on grounds of religion or belief' and, as we have seen, 'religion or belief' is defined as meaning 'any religion, religious belief, or similar philosophical belief.'

An extremely important question, in terms of the scope of the Regulations, is whether it allows employers to discriminate in favour of those who share their own religion or belief and, conversely, whether it protects people from being discriminated against not merely because of what they believe, but also because of their lack of a particular belief.

If a Muslim employer, for instance, decides it will only employ someone who is Muslim, can those who were turned down because they were not Muslim claim that they were discriminated against because of their religious belief? Does it make a difference whether those who were turned down hold a particular religious or philosophical belief, or does the protection of the law extend to those who have no particular beliefs or who are uncertain? Let us be clear about this: if the Regulations do not protect those who are discriminated against because they do not hold a particular belief, there is a major gap in the statutory protection.

An argument could be made that there is nothing wrong with discriminating in favour of co-religionists and that freedom of religion or belief includes a general right to associate with and employ others of the same religion or belief. This is definitely not the approach taken by the Government. It is clear that the Government intended to protect non-believers against discrimination on grounds of their absence of belief. The ACAS Guide unequivocally takes the position that the Regulations cover those who are not religious or who do not subscribe to a particular belief. In discussing the meaning of 'religion or belief', the Guide says: 'The Regulations also cover those without religious or similar beliefs.' The DTI explanatory notes take the same position and explain the Government's reasoning in more detail: 'references to "religious belief" and "similar philosophical belief" include reference to an individual's belief structure involving the absence of particular beliefs because these are two sides of the same coin … For example, if a Christian employer refuses an individual a job because he is not Christian, regardless of whether he is Muslim, Hindu, atheist

(etc), that would be direct discrimination on grounds of the individual's religious belief, which can be described as "non-Christian". It is not necessary to identify the individual as an atheist or a Hindu for the purposes of the Regulations in such circumstances if he can be identified as a "non-Christian". The same is true of persons who might describe themselves as "unconcerned" by religious beliefs, or "unsure" of them.'

There is some superficial support for the DTI's position from the Kokkinakis case mentioned above, where the European Court of Human Rights gave the following characterisation of 'freedom of thought, conscience and religion': 'It is in its religious dimension one of the most vital elements that go to make up the identity of believers and their conception of life, but it is also a precious asset for atheists, sceptics and the unconcerned.' On analysis, however, the ECHR here may not be treating 'unconcerned' as some sort of religious belief. Instead, a better reading of this passage is that the Human Rights Court is making the straightforward point that all people, religious or not, value the right to freedom of thought and conscience (as well as of religion).

In any event, it is difficult to reconcile the DTI's reasoning on this point with the guidance that it has given as to the meaning of a 'religion or belief' in the Regulations. 'Non-Christian' is not a 'religious belief'. 'Unsure' or 'don't know' cannot be regarded as a 'profound belief affecting a person's way of life or perception of the world'.

Because the legislation was introduced by way of Regulations, it could not be amended when it became apparent that this was a serious source of concern. Whether absence of belief was protected was one of the key issues probed during the House of Lords debate on the Regulations on 17 June 2003. The Government spokesman, Lord Sainsbury, said that: 'It is clearly the intention that where people have strongly held views, which include humanism, or atheism or agnosticism, they would be covered under the phrase "or similar philosophical belief".' Yet this is a rather different point, which far from providing Parliamentary support for the proposition that discrimination on grounds of non-belief is covered tends to undermine the argument: it is clear that the Regulations cover someone who is discriminated against because of their strongly held view such as atheism. What is not clear is whether the Regulations cover someone who is discriminated against because of their weakly-held view, ie who is 'unsure' or, more importantly, whether they cover someone who is discriminated against because they do not share the discriminator's religious views.

Much religious discrimination takes the guise of discrimination in favour of co-religionists or those who share the discriminator's belief, rather than being against those of a particular religion. As discussed below, the Regulations contain special provisions allowing positive discrimination in the form of genuine occupational requirements, so a liberal construction by a tribunal would find that someone discriminated against because of their absence of belief would fall within the scope of the Regulations unless a GOR is established. It is to be hoped that this is the way the Regulations will be interpreted, for otherwise there will be a major gap in the protection offered.

It has to be said that the Government could have avoided any uncertainty by specifically providing that absence of belief fell within the definition of discrimination. This is what was done in the Fair Employment (Northern Ireland) Act 1976, s 57(2) of which provides: 'In this Act references to a person's religious belief or political opinion include references to his supposed religious belief or political opinion and to the absence or supposed absence of any, or any particular, religious belief or political opinion.' Similarly, the Anti-terrorism, Crime and Security Act 2001, s 39 which created the offence of religiously aggravated harassment, defines "religious group" as meaning 'a group of persons defined by reference to religious belief or lack of religious belief.'

The fact that the drafters of the Religion or Belief Regulations did not choose to follow the language in two cases where the legislation is so closely comparable will be a powerful argument to a court construing the Regulations that they were not intended to cover absence or lack of belief.

It follows that whether someone is protected because of an absence of belief will be a key issue

that will have to be determined by the tribunals. However, because we know that the Government intended to cover non-believers, most of the remainder of this chapter is drafted on the assumption that non-believers are protected.

Rights of non-believers

The corollary of the premise that non-believers have a right not to be discriminated against on grounds of their absence of belief is that believers do not have a right to more favourable treatment because of their beliefs.

Much of the practical advice on avoiding religious discrimination has been couched in terms of the need to accommodate the beliefs and practices associated with particular religious groups. This advice is helpful and some of it is discussed below. Good employers will wish to make adjustments to meet the needs associated with their employees' religious beliefs, and if they do not do so, they may well risk a claim of indirect discrimination. But if they do so, employers will have to take care that they do not end up by discriminating directly against other employees.

Take a classic religious discrimination issue: an employer that institutes Sunday working. Mr X, backed by the Keep Sunday Special campaign, uses the new Regulations to request Sunday off in order to go to church. If the employer grants the request merely because of its religious connotations, it may find itself in difficulties under the Regulations if it turns down the request of Ms Y, who looks after her sick mother on Sundays because no one else in her family is available to do so, or even if it turns down the request for Sundays off from Mr Z, who has a regular football game in the park. If Mr X is given Sunday off because of his religious belief, it is strongly arguable that Ms Y and Mr Z are being treated less favourably on grounds of their lack of religious belief.

Direct discrimination

The Regulations define direct discrimination as follows:

'3(1) For the purposes of these Regulations, a person ("A") discriminates against another person ("B") if—

(a) on grounds of religion or belief, A treats B less favourably than he treats or would treat other persons.'

It is clear that this definition is framed so as to cover perceived discrimination: where the discrimination is based on the discriminator's perception of a person's religion or belief even if that perception is not accurate. Thus, someone who was discriminated against because they 'looked Jewish' would have a claim under the Regulations regardless of whether or not they actually were Jewish. Similarly, if an employer rejected an applicant because they needed someone to work on Friday and they assumed that the applicant would not because they had a Muslim name. There is no requirement that a worker has to follow a religion in order to be protected against being discriminated against on grounds of that religion.

The Regulations also cover discrimination by association, and discrimination for refusing to follow an instruction to discriminate.

Discriminator's belief not covered

In practice, the problem of absence of belief discussed above could have been avoided if the wording of the consultative draft Regulations had not been altered. Because the definition of direct discrimination simply refers to less favourable treatment 'on grounds of religion or belief', reg 3(1), on its own, would allow a claim where the discrimination was on grounds of the religion or belief of A, the discriminator, as well as where it was on grounds of B's religion or belief. That would have clearly covered the situation where an employer discriminates on grounds of religion in favour of his or her co-religionists.

However, it may well also have covered a situation where an employer, because of his or her religious beliefs, discriminates against someone because of their sexual orientation. This is clearly potentially

actionable under the Sexual Orientation Regulations, because it is B's sexual orientation that leads to her or him being treated less favourably than someone of a different sexual orientation. But, as is well known, the Government took a late decision to permit such discrimination in certain circumstances by adding a genuine occupational requirement exclusion to the Sexual Orientation Regulations. It also added a further provision to the Religion or Belief Regulations, reg 3(2), which stipulates that discrimination on grounds of religion or belief 'does not include A's religion or belief', ie the religion or belief of the discriminator.

According to the explanatory notes, this was included 'for the avoidance of doubt'. The DTI takes the position that 'an employer with strong religious views who refuses to employ an applicant because she is female or gay does not discriminate on grounds of religion or belief. The cause of the difference of treatment, objectively considered, is the sex or sexual orientation of the applicant. The employer's religious views are not the cause of the difference of treatment; an employer without such views might refuse to employ a female or gay applicant in exactly the same way. The motivation for the act of discrimination (whether religious or otherwise) is not relevant.'

There is much in this assertion by the DTI that is at least open to question. Where an employer will not employ someone who is, for example, not white and British, the straightforward interpretation is that this is because of the employer's racist views rather than the particular nationality and colour of the person discriminated against. Moreover, whilst it is clear that a 'good' motive will not excuse discrimination, it does not follow that a discriminatory motive is irrelevant. Although the courts have used that phrase on several occasions, it has always been in the context of asserting that what is otherwise discrimination is not saved from illegality by the benign motive of the discriminator. On the other hand, proof that the employer was impelled by racism, religious bigotry or homophobia should be sufficient to show that the treatment in question was on grounds of race, religion or sexual orientation as the case may be.

The stipulation that the religion or belief of the putative discriminator must not be taken into account may well give rise to difficult arguments about whether a person has been discriminated against because of their own religious views, or lack of them, or whether the real reason was the employer's beliefs and that this has the result that any discrimination falls outside the scope of the Regulations.

Suppose a Roman Catholic employer with strong religious views dismisses an employee when he finds out that she is having a relationship with a married man. That treatment is clearly on the grounds of the employer's religion or belief, but it is far-fetched to treat it as being on grounds of some sort of belief – or lack of it – by the employee dismissed. A more likely finding is that this will fall outside the scope of the Regulations altogether, narrowing its protection.

Indirect discrimination

The definition of indirect discrimination and the general principles relating to its proof were discussed in the first part of this book.

One of the issues that may complicate potential cases of indirect discrimination on grounds of religion or belief is that unlike sex or sexual orientation, for example, an individual may belong to a range of religious or belief groups. For example, one might be a Christian, a Protestant, belong to the Church of England, and be a member of an evangelical church. The same person might even be a pacifist and a vegan as well.

The position will be even more complicated if the DTI is correct in its interpretation that non-belief is a religion or belief group for the purposes of the Regulations. The DTI explanatory notes say: 'the complainant's relevant religion or belief group may be identified in two ways. That is because it is possible that the complainant's religion or belief may be identified as being (for example) Jewish or atheist on the one hand, or "non-Muslim" on the other … .In whichever way the complainant describes his beliefs, he must establish that the relevant group of persons with those beliefs is put at a particular disadvantage.'

Genuine occupational requirement

Article 4 of the Framework Employment Directive allows Member States to provide that a difference in treatment based on religion or belief, sexual orientation, disability or age shall not constitute discrimination 'where by reason of the nature of the particular occupational activities concerned or of the context in which they are carried out, such a characteristic constitutes a genuine and determining occupational requirement, provided that the objective is legitimate and the requirement is proportionate.'

In essence, therefore, this allows discrimination to be justified by the nature of the work in question. So far as religious discrimination is concerned, the Directive contains a specific derogation allowing differences of treatment based on a person's religion or belief, where this is in respect of employment by 'churches or other public or private organisations the ethos of which is based on religion or belief', and this is a 'genuine, legitimate and justified occupational requirement having regard to the organisation's ethos.' The Directive adds that: 'Provided that its provisions are otherwise complied with, this Directive shall thus not prejudice the right of churches and other public or private organisations, the ethos of which is based on religion or belief, acting in conformity with national constitutions and laws, to require individuals working for them to act in good faith and with loyalty to the organisation's ethos.'

The Regulations implement these derogations by providing for two separate genuine occupational requirement (GOR) exceptions: a general one based on the nature of the work in question, and a more specific exception based on the nature of the employer's organisation and limited to employers whose ethos is based on religion or belief.

The general GOR is set out in reg 7(2). It says that the provisions relating to discrimination in recruitment, promotion, transfer, training or dismissal do not apply:

'where, having regard to the nature of the employment or the context in which it is carried out—

(a) being of a particular religion or belief is a genuine and determining occupational requirement;

(b) it is proportionate to apply that requirement in the particular case; and

(c) either –

    (i) the person to whom the requirement is applied does not meet it, or

    (ii) the employer is not satisfied, and in all the circumstances it is reasonable for him not to be satisfied, that that person meets it

and this paragraph applies whether or not the employer has an ethos based on religion or belief.'

Regulation 7(3) then goes on to make the burden of establishing a genuine occupational requirement easier for an ethos-based organisation in that being of a particular religion or belief does not have to be a 'determining' occupational requirement. It will be sufficient if it is 'genuine'. This is discussed in more detail below.

Note that reg 7 may apply where an employer is dismissing a person from a post. This is intended to cater for the situation in which, after taking up a post to which a GOR applies, an employee's religion changes, such as where they convert to a different religion. If they then no longer meet the GOR in question, they would no longer be able to perform the functions of the post and, accordingly, the employer would be justified in dismissing.

General GOR: genuine and determining requirement

In the ordinary case, an employer must show that being of a particular religion or belief is both a 'genuine' and a 'determining' occupational requirement having regard to the 'nature of the employment' or 'the context in which it is carried out'.

The first limb of this definition can be satisfied by a showing that the GOR is genuine and determining either because of the nature of the employment

itself and/or because of the wider context in which it is carried out. The DTI explanatory notes give the following example: 'one could describe the functions of a counsellor in a Christian support group for people with long-term illnesses in a very narrow sense as simply talking with and advising the people involved. On this view (which would be misleading), a person of any religion or belief could perform those functions if they could offer appropriate advice. But when considering the *context* of the job, it is self-evident that the person must be Christian in order to carry out the job, because the purpose of the job is to provide advice from a Christian perspective.'

Not everyone will agree with this as an illustration of a 'self-evident' GOR, especially on the DTI's premise that someone of a different religion could also offer 'appropriate advice'. It is, of course, open to the support group to recruit someone who is not only able to give appropriate advice, but also advice from a Christian perspective, but it does not necessarily follow that only a practising Christian will be able to meet this criterion. It may well be that few or no non-Christians will apply for the job, or that if they did, that they would not be the best candidate if they were put through the normal selection process. It is not fanciful, however, to imagine a non-Christian well-versed in a Christian perspective, perhaps because they once were deeply Christian, or through study or through association with others, who would be able to meet the standard required. The same reasoning may be applicable to jobs with organisations advising lesbians and gay men. Indeed, this principle is acknowledged by the DTI at a different place in its explanatory notes: 'in many jobs, it will be sufficient that employees have some understanding of, and respect for, the religion or belief in question, or persons of the particular sexual orientation, as the case may be. If that is the case, then being of that particular sexual orientation/ religion or belief would not be a genuine occupational requirement for the job.'

As a derogation from the principle of equal treatment, the genuine occupational requirement exceptions must be construed narrowly, and it may well be that tribunals will take a less permissive view of this than the DTI.

In order to fit within reg 7(2)(a), it must be shown that there is an occupational requirement that is genuine and determining. The DTI explanatory notes suggest that:

'• A *requirement* is stronger than something which is merely a factor, a preference or a qualification for the job – it is something which is essential for the person to be able to perform the functions of the job.
• It must also be a *determining* requirement – that is, the requirement must be crucial to the post, and not merely one of several important factors.
• The fact that it must be an *occupational* requirement emphasises the necessary connection to the job in question.
• And it must be a *genuine* occupational requirement for that job – in other words the employer cannot simply create a requirement on a whim because he does not like persons of a particular sexual orientation/religion or belief.'

The DTI acknowledges that it is 'rare for a particular religion or belief to be a genuine occupational requirement for a job under reg 7(2) of the Religion or Belief Regulations. In the vast majority of jobs, a person's religion or belief has no bearing on whether or not they can perform the functions of the job in question.' The DTI gives as a further possible example for where a GOR could operate, a post as a chaplain in a hospital: 'if a hospital were to employ a chaplain to minister to patients and staff, it might specify that he or she must be Christian, because almost all the patients and staff are Christian. If the patients and staff represented a number of different faiths, the hospital might need to give consideration to whether a minister of another faith could also carry out the job, including ministering to those of faiths other than his or her own. Even in that case, the hospital could probably specify that the chaplain must be a minister of a religion, rather than an atheist, for example.'

Proportionate

In order for an employer to establish a GOR, the Regulations require that it is 'proportionate' to apply the requirement in the particular case.

We explored the meaning of the word 'proportionate' in the context of indirect discrimination earlier in this book. The DTI takes the view that the word has the same meaning in both contexts:

'for the application of the requirement to be proportionate means that it must be an appropriate and necessary means of achieving the legitimate aim in question – namely that the employer needs to recruit a person able to perform the functions of the job ... generally, an appropriate means is one which is suitable to achieve the aim in question, and which actually does so. A necessary means is one without which the aim could not be achieved; it is not simply a convenient means. This will include consideration of whether the aim could be achieved by other means which have lesser discriminatory effects.'

The DTI's interpretation is interesting because it might be argued that the test for establishing a genuine occupational requirement, since it is a derogation from the principle of equal treatment, is stricter than that for establishing justification for indirect discrimination. At any rate, it is certainly not a looser test.

The sections of the Sex Discrimination Act on genuine occupational qualifications include the principle that a GOQ cannot be established in respect of filling a vacancy where the employer already has other employees of that sex who could reasonably carry out those duties. The same principle can be regarded as applicable to whether it would be proportionate to exclude persons of a particular religion, belief or sexual orientation.

Meeting the genuine occupational requirement

Regulation 7(2)(c) provides that the GOR exception can apply either where the employee or job applicant does not meet the requirement, or where 'the employer is not satisfied, and in all the circumstances it is reasonable for him not to be satisfied' that the employee or applicant meets the requirement.

Unlike a person's sex and (usually) their race, someone's religion or belief (or their sexual orientation) are not usually evident. The reason for reg 7(2)(c) is that without some such provision, an employer might only be able to determine whether someone held the requisite belief by detailed questioning. Writing on the Regulations in the *Industrial Law Journal*, 'The Employment Equality (Religion or Belief) Regulations 2003', September 2003), Lucy Vickers says: 'A person could claim, in good faith, to be of a particular religion (for example he could be baptised into the Christian church, but not be a believer). An employer may disagree, based on poor performance in interview when questioned about faith matters. Without this additional clause it was not clear how an employer could determine whether the person does not comply with the requirement set. The additional clause would also help in cases where the question of whether the applicant complies with the faith is determined by fine theological judgements, on which even the parties do not agree. Again, the applicant may be of the view that they comply, but the employer may disagree. In such circumstances, regs 7(2)(c) and (3)(c) allows the matter to be determined by the employer, as long as in the circumstances the assessment is reasonable.'

If the matter is in dispute, the burden will be on the employer to satisfy one or other limb. This is more likely to be an issue as regards discrimination on grounds of sexual orientation, and the question is discussed in detail in that chapter. In the context of religious discrimination, it might permit an employer with a Roman Catholic ethos, for example, to reject an applicant who was divorced on the basis of a reasonable belief that they were not Catholic, even though the individual concerned might continue to define themselves as a Catholic.

Religious ethos

An employer that has a religious ethos has an easier task in establishing a genuine occupational requirement. Regulation 7(3) provides:

'This paragraph applies where an employer has an ethos based on religion or belief and, having regard to that ethos and to the nature of the employment or the context in which it is carried out—

(a) being of a particular religion or belief is a genuine occupational requirement for the job; and

(b) it is proportionate to apply that requirement in the particular case; and

(c) either –

(i) the person to whom the requirement is applied does not meet it, or

(ii) the employer is not satisfied, and in all the circumstances it is reasonable for him not to be satisfied, that that person meets it.'

Thus, the wording of reg 7(2) and (3) is almost the same. In both cases, the employer must show that being of a particular religion or belief is a genuine occupational requirement for the job, and that it is proportionate to apply that requirement in the particular case. In the case of an employer that can establish that it has an ethos-based religion or belief, however, it is not necessary to also show that being of particular religion or belief is a 'determining' – or decisive – occupational requirement for the post in question. Instead, it will be sufficient that being of a particular religion is a 'genuine' requirement. However, the employer must still show that the religion or belief is a requirement, and, as the DTI puts it, not 'just one of many relevant factors.'

The onus will be on the employer to show that it has an ethos based on religion or belief. What evidence will be accepted by tribunals? The DTI explanatory notes suggest that the employer 'may seek to rely on evidence such as the organisation's founding constitution or similar documents, provisions in contracts of employment used by the employer, or other evidence about the practices of the employer's organisation and the way it is run.'

This still leaves open questions as to what organisations will be regarded as ethos-based and for which jobs will it be considered proportionate to apply a genuine occupational requirement. The criteria of an employer having 'an ethos based on religion or belief' is clearly broader than that of an 'organised religion' as used in the Sexual Orientation

Regulations (see below). In addition to religious organisations as such, the definition is likely to extend to church-run schools, hospitals and care homes. It might also, in certain cases, extend to 'Christian' or 'Jewish' or 'Muslim' law firms or medical practices. What about organisations who have an ethos based on belief? Would this allow, for example, an abortion advisory service to exclude opponents of abortion from certain posts? What of the vegan restaurant or the pacifist book shop?

The burden is on the employer to establish that applying a genuine occupational requirement is 'proportionate' as regards a particular job. The DTI explanatory notes suggest: 'In practice, if an employer with a religious ethos already employs a person who does not have the required religion or belief in a particular post, this will provide a very strong indication that having that religion or belief is not a GOR for the post.'

A key issue will be the range of jobs an ethos-based employer will be allowed to designate as having a GOR. It is arguable that the requirement that the GOR must be 'proportionate' should be interpreted as meaning that religious exclusions apply only to particular posts where the religion or belief is relevant, rather than to all the jobs in the organisation. The DTI explanatory notes take this view: 'in practice, a GOR will apply to a job for an employer with an ethos based on religion or belief only in a small number of cases. A GOR is more likely to apply if the job is one that has particular importance for maintaining the ethos of the employer's organisation.' The ACAS Guide adopts a rather stricter stance: 'Where the organisation has a religious ethos, a GOR exemption cannot be claimed if the nature of the role and the context within which it is carried out is not of sufficient profile or impact within the organisation to affect the overall ethos of the organisation.' On that basis, one would ask what the effect would be if the job was filled by someone not of the particular religion or belief?

Whichever is the correct test, however, it is unlikely that a GOR will be regarded as existing for all the jobs in a particular organisation, so that applicants who do not share the organisation's religious ethos

could be routinely excluded. The DTI gives two examples in this connection:

'a Christian hospice could probably show that it was a requirement for its chief executive to adhere to that faith, because of the leadership which a chief executive must give in relation to maintaining and developing the religious ethos. It could only establish that a similar requirement applied to a nurse in the hospice if there were aspects of the job or its context going beyond the medical care of patients which required that the person must adhere to the particular faith.

On the other hand, it would not be a GOR for a shop assistant to be of a particular faith in order to work in a bookshop with a religious ethos, if for all practical purposes the nature and context of the job are the same as for a shop assistant in any other bookshop. The fact that the employer or customers may prefer a person of the same faith is not relevant to whether or not a GOR applies to the job.'

It is interesting that the similar example given in the ACAS Guide has a different emphasis: 'A faith based care home may be able to show that being of a particular faith is a genuine requirement of its carers because they are required to carry out their duties in a manner that fulfils both the physical and spiritual needs of its patients. However, they may not be able to justify a similar requirement for their maintenance or receptions staff whose jobs do not require them to provide spiritual leadership or support to the patients.'

The relevant ethos for the purposes of establishing a GOR may relate to a religion or a belief, or both. Indeed, the DTI explanatory notes refer to 'adherence to a religion' and 'a specific belief based in that religion', suggesting that this is unlikely to found a GOR 'unless the belief has particular relevance to the nature or context of the job.' The DTI uses the example of the chief executive of a Christian hospice with an ethos not only based on Christianity, 'but more specifically on Christian beliefs to the effect that gay sex is not acceptable.' According to the DTI, 'it would only be a GOR for the chief executive to hold those beliefs, if the nature or context of the job required it.'

The DTI rightly goes on to warn that the hospice might be risking a claim under the Sexual Orientation Regulations if it applied such a requirement, but the example raises yet again a question as to the correct interpretation of the statutory language. If a Christian 'belief' that gay sex is not acceptable is a 'belief' which the employer can rely upon, in appropriate circumstances under the Religion or Belief Regulations to discriminate against a gay employee in recruitment or even in dismissing him, why is it not a 'belief' that a Christian employee can rely upon under the Religion or Belief Regulations when they express that view to a gay colleague and are disciplined for it?

A case example which is frequently discussed in the context of the new Regulations is *O'Neill v Governors of St Thomas More RCVA Upper School* [1996] IRLR 372. This was the case of a teacher of religious education and personal relationships at a Roman Catholic school who was dismissed when she became pregnant, and it was discovered that the father was a local Roman Catholic priest. The EAT held that the dismissal was on grounds of pregnancy, and therefore on grounds of sex, and unlawfully discriminatory. Such a dismissal, on the facts of the case, almost certainly would be permissible under the Religion or Belief Regulations. The analysis probably is that the school falls under the School Standards and Framework Act 1998 (see below) and the conduct would be regarded as incompatible with the school's religious character. It by no means follows, however, that this would alter the reasoning that the dismissal was sex discrimination, although one suspects that the courts would strive mightily to avoid such a result in light of the new legislation and, in any event, the 'but for' test of causation used in *O'Neill* is no longer applied.

Faith-based schools

Article 4(2) of the Directive allows ethos-based organisations to 'require individuals working for them to act in good faith and with loyalty to the organisation's ethos.' The Government did not

transpose this 'loyalty' requirement into the Regulations, but a similar rule is allowed to apply to teachers in faith-based schools.

The School Standards and Framework Act 1998 prevents discrimination against existing teachers and applicants for positions on the basis of their religious opinions or attendance at worship. However, this protection does not apply to Voluntary Aided schools or independent schools with a 'religious character'.

Schools with a 'religious character' are allowed to give preference to teachers who have religious opinions in accordance with the tenets of the religion or religious denomination specified in relation to the school, or who attend religious worship in accordance with those tenets, or have a willingness to give religious education in accordance with those tenets. The Act also provides that in terminating a teacher's employment, schools may have regard to 'any conduct which is incompatible with the precepts, or with the upholding of the tenets, of the religion or religious denomination' concerned.

This is unaffected by the Religion or Belief Regulations, and indeed these provisions were extended to independent schools in 2003 by the Independent Schools (Employment of Teachers in Schools with a Religious Character) Regulations. During 2003, prior to the discrimination Regulations coming into force, the Department for Education and Skills sent out a circular encouraging schools to register their religious character.

The Scottish equivalent of this legislation, the Education (Scotland) Act 1980, requires that any person appointed to the staff of a denominational school must be approved as regards religious belief and character by representatives of the relevant church or denominational body.

Although the Framework Employment Directive allows Member States to give ethos-based organisations a fair degree of discretion, any genuine occupational requirement must be 'genuine, legitimate and justified' by reason of the nature of the occupational activities or the context in which it is carried out. The School Standards and Framework Act 1998, and its Scottish equivalent, are not restricted to any particular teaching posts for which holding a particular religious belief can be regarded as 'genuine, legitimate and justified'. They allow preference to be given purely on the basis of holding religious beliefs, even if the post could be done equally well by a candidate with different beliefs. They allow discrimination against the peripatetic music teacher in the same way as the head of religious studies. It must be doubtful whether this comports with the requirements of the Directive.

Recruitment

Regulation 6 makes it unlawful for employers to discriminate against on grounds of religion or belief (or harass) applicants for employment at an establishment in Great Britain. The scope of this is in identical language to the scope of the Race Relations Act and the Sexual Orientation Regulations. It covers selection arrangements, the terms on which employment is offered and refusing to offer employment.

So far as arrangements for selection are concerned, the ACAS Guide recommends that 'where it is reasonable to do so, organisations should adapt their methods of recruitment so that anyone who is suitably qualified can apply and attend for selection. Some flexibility around interview/selection times allowing avoidance of significant religious times (for example Friday afternoons) is good practice.'

Arguably, this is understating the position. An organisation that fails to adapt its methods of recruitment with the result that suitably qualified applicants are unable to attend interviews because of a conflict with their religious beliefs is indirectly discriminating. Whatever precise legal standard of justification is adopted by the courts, it is clear that it will be more demanding than whether it was 'reasonable' for the employer to adapt its methods of recruitment. As we saw in the chapter on indirect discrimination, the employer in such a case will have to show that it was both 'appropriate and necessary' to hold the interviews on Friday afternoon.

The ACAS Guide is more helpful when it points out that: 'Where the recruitment process includes a social

gathering, care should be taken to avoid disadvantaging anyone for whom alcohol is prohibited on the grounds of religion or belief. For instance, holding the gathering in a hotel bar may pose particular difficulties for those whose religion forbids association with alcohol.'

Questions should be avoided during interviews which ask about place or frequency of worship, communal involvement or the religious ethos of educational establishments attended.

Training

Training, including training outside normal working hours and away from the normal place of work, may need to be adapted to avoid disadvantaging an employee because of their religion or belief. The ACAS Guide recommends as things to consider:

'• times within work schedules for religious observance
• special dietary requirements, for example kosher, halal and vegetarian food
• avoid ice breakers and training activities that use language or physical contact that might be inappropriate for some beliefs
• avoid exercises which require the exchange of personal information
• ensure related social activities do not exclude people by choice of venue
• avoid significant religious festivals such as Ramadan.'

Harassment

Harassment on grounds of religion or belief is made specifically unlawful by the Regulations. The definition used is similar to that for the other strands covered by the new Regulations. We looked at the general issue of harassment in the first part of this book. Note that the harassment provisions, unlike the provisions on direct discrimination, do not provide that 'religion or belief' does not include the perpetrator's religion or belief. Therefore, they clearly cover harassment of someone because they do not share the harasser's belief.

From a practical standpoint, providing a remedy against Islamophobia (see below) is likely to be the most important function of the bar on harassment on grounds of religion or belief. However, there are a number of other circumstances where a person's religion or beliefs can lead to them being bullied or harassed, ranging from sectarian rivalries linked with football clubs, to anti-Semitism, to namecalling of members of cult religions, or teasing of those with particular beliefs.

Faith at work

In the US, it is becoming increasingly common for employees to bring their faith into work by holding Bible study classes and prayer groups.

There are major differences between the US and the UK in terms of approach to religion: according to opinion polls, 55% of Americans regularly attend a religious service, whereas the comparable figure for the British is only 18%. Nevertheless, British workplaces have their share of evangelicals, for whom religion cannot be 'left at home'. As Michael Skapinker pointed out in an article in the *Financial Times* ('Save us from edge-of-the seat religious experiences', 18 February 2004), 'the champions of faith-at-work argue that they are simply part of the growing diversity movement. If gay employees no longer have to hide who they are, why should churchgoers? If black employees can form support organisations at work, why shouldn't Christians do so, too?'

Employers implementing the new Regulations will have to balance the right of evangelicals to express their beliefs at work with ensuring that the views expressed do not create a working environment which is offensive for others who do not share those views.

Where a religious employee attempts to proselytise others at work and they regard this as unwanted harassment, is the employer risking losing a religious discrimination complaint if he attempts to silence the proselytiser? It could be argued that such an employee is exercising their Convention right to manifest their religion, but the Convention right is itself limited, according to Article 9, where this is

necessary 'for the protection of the rights and freedoms of others.'

Employers have a duty to uphold the rights of their employees not to be subjected to harassment and that duty cannot depend on whether the harasser is impelled by their own religious convictions. This suggests that tribunals will uphold employer restrictions on expressing religious views where the expression has caused offence to others.

Conversely, however, employees with strong religious beliefs may be offended by a workplace that is sexualised, or by open discussion of sexual experiences, or by use of blasphemous or obscene language. For some Christian employees, expressions such as 'Oh my God' or 'Jesus Christ' are offensive. In this context, it is important to bear in mind the precise definition of the test for unlawful harassment on grounds of religion or belief. Although reg 5(2) says that conduct will only be regarded as having the effect of violating the employee's dignity or creating an intimidating, hostile, degrading or offensive environment if 'having regard to all the circumstances, including in particular the perception of B, it should reasonably be considered as having that effect', this proviso as to the employee's reasonable reaction does not apply where that can be inferred to have been the purpose of the conduct. Thus, if a tribunal finds that a religious employee's colleagues deliberately discussed their sexual experiences in front of her in order to embarrass her, this should lead to a finding that the purpose of the unwanted conduct was to violate the employee's dignity or to create an offensive working environment. In such a case, the harassment will be unlawful discrimination regardless of whether the employee's reaction could be characterised as reasonable.

Jokes about religion, or use of blasphemous or obscene language, may be common in some workplaces. Some religious employees who are offended by such conduct may have gone along with it without protest until now because they had no legal remedy. Employers will need to ensure that their dignity and harassment policies extend to religious discrimination issues and that employees are made aware that their behaviour may cause offence.

Football rivalries

The new law relating to religious harassment will also be relevant in workplaces where football club allegiances serve as a proxy for sectarian rivalry. This is particularly the case in the West of Scotland between Glasgow Rangers and Glasgow Celtic supporters. In Northern Ireland, where support for Rangers and Celtic divides on sectarian lines also, it has long been acknowledged that the display in the workplace of football emblems, such as scarves and badges, which have a sectarian significance can create an offensive working environment.

In *Brennan v Short Bros plc* (20 September 1995), the Fair Employment Tribunal for Northern Ireland held that regalia and apparel, such as Rangers and Celtic shirts and scarves, give clear sectarian messages in Northern Ireland. 'If football shirts have a sectarian significance, they are not simply football shirts, regardless of the intention with which they are worn. It has to be emphasised as often as is necessary that anything which identifies community allegiance needs justification in the workplace.'

Islamophobia

Muslims are the major British group brought within the scope of protection against discrimination and harassment at work by the new Regulations.

The problem of Islamophobia – a prejudice against Muslims as a group – has been well-documented by the European Monitoring Centre on Racism and Xenophobia (see the 2002 UK report by the Commission for Racial Equality, 'Anti-Islamic reactions in the EU after the terrorist attacks against the USA' prepared for *Summary Report on Islamophobia in the EU after 11 September 2001*). There is clear evidence that Islamophobia has been exacerbated in reaction to international terrorism and Islamic extremists. There is no doubt that Islamic extremists, preaching a message of intolerance, exist in Britain, but they are usually found in the mosques, not in the workplace. Islamophobia wrongly lumps these extremists together with the tolerant majority of British Muslims.

The ACAS guide adopts a remarkably coy approach to this issue, as if to mention the very word 'Muslim' would itself give validity to the discrimination: 'A particular religion featured largely in the media due to an international crisis. Stereotypical, pejorative and hurtful comments in the workplace were routinely made about all followers of that religion. A group of distressed workers complained to managers who promptly arranged a training session during which it was explained that not all followers of that religion agreed with what was happening elsewhere and that they were hurt and worried by their colleagues' comments. Better understanding helped to resolve the situation.'

Any employer wishing to comply with the Religion or Belief Regulations will take steps to ensure that harassment policies clearly cover Islamophobia and that employees understand what this entails.

Anti-Semitism

Attention has recently focused on what is seen as a resurgence of anti-Semitism. In recent years, there has been a rise in attacks against Jews and Jewish properties in Western Europe, including the UK. A report commissioned by the EU's European Monitoring Centre on Racism and Xenophobia by Professor Werner Bergmann and Dr Julianne Wetzel (*Manifestations of anti-Semitism in the European Union*, February 2003) found that these attacks were 'committed above all either by right-wing extremists or radical Islamists or young Muslims mostly of Arab descent.' The report generated controversy because it was not initially published by the Monitoring Centre. The Centre claimed that this was because of technical deficiencies, but others have alleged that it was because it linked attacks on Jews to Muslims.

Often, but not always, underlying the new anti-Semitism is sympathy for the Palestinian cause and antagonism towards the state of Israel. In Britain, this is a view that can be shared by elements of the new Left and is also often associated with anti-Americanism. Anti-Zionism is not anti-Semitism as such, still less does criticism of the current policies of the Israeli Government equate to anti-Semitism.

Nevertheless, the line between anti-Zionism and anti-Semitism is often blurry. Jews can be harassed because of their support for Israel or because no distinction is drawn between their Jewishness and perceived support for Israel, as the EUMC report found.

In the UK, anti-Semitism often takes the form of attributing disproportionate power to Jews. A poll carried out by ICM Research published in January 2004 found that 18% agreed with the statement that 'Jews have too much influence in this country', whereas 47% disagreed, 25% were neutral and 10% said they did not know. When the Labour MP Tam Dalyell, writing in *Vanity Fair* in May 2003, accused Tony Blair of 'being unduly influenced' by Jews, this provoked little media reaction.

To the extent that views such as these are allowed to enter the workplace, they can result in a working environment that is felt by Jewish employees to be hostile.

Work requirements and working conditions

The ACAS Guide suggests that 'organisations do not have to employ people whose beliefs mean that they are unable to undertake essential parts of the job. It should be made clear to candidates what type of work the organisation does and what duties the job involves so they can consider whether there is any chance it might conflict with their religion or beliefs.'

This seems a matter of common sense. Where the position is more complicated is if religion or belief acts as a constraint as regards only a small part of the employee's duties. The best way of viewing this might be to view it as equivalent to a reverse genuine occupational requirement: ie whether *not* being of a particular religious or belief group is, in effect, a GOR for the job in question. That allows account to be taken of whether it is reasonable for duties to be allocated so that the employee is able to undertake the job consistently with their religion or belief. ACAS appears to be taking such an approach in the examples its guide gives: 'An individual applying for a

job in a large supermarket stacking shelves may not be willing to handle pork products for religious reasons. Such products probably represent only a small proportion of the goods displayed on the shelves. It may not be reasonable to reject such job applicants if it is practicable to allocate work in a way that does not involve handling pork products. However, it may not be practical for the store to adjust the work of a check-out operative in order that they are not required to handle pork products.'

A real life example was reported in the *Daily Mail* on 5 February 2004 of an in-store pharmacist employed by Asda who refused to sell a woman the morning-after contraceptive pill because it was against his religious beliefs as a devout Christian. The employers in this case are quoted as having taken the view that 'we cannot force a colleague to sell a product that goes against their religious or moral beliefs.' This appears to be in accord with the code of ethics and standards set out by the Royal Pharmaceutical Society, which states that where a pharmacist's religious beliefs prevent them from providing a service, they must advise patients of alternative sources for the service requested. That was said to have been done by the pharmacist in this case.

Some people might object on grounds associated with their religion to being required to share an office or a workplace with someone else of a different religion, or who is gay, or a woman, for that matter. Although such requirements might be regarded as prima facie indirectly discriminatory on grounds of religion or belief, it is highly likely that they would be held to be proportionate and justified. The general rule is that maintaining a religious principle is not lawful if it results in discrimination against others on grounds of their religion, sexual orientation, disability, race or sex.

Shower and changing facilities

Same-sex communal shower and changing facilities disadvantage those whose religion or belief does not allow them to undress or shower in the company of others, even of the same sex. This could present an indirect discrimination issue if the employer requires its staff, for reasons of health and safety, to change their clothing or shower.

Prayer rooms

When the Regulations were first mooted, much was written about how this might require employers to set aside rooms for prayer for observant Muslims and others.

The ACAS Guide takes the view 'employers are not required to provide a prayer room. However, if a quiet place is available and allowing its use for prayer does not cause problems for other workers or the business, organisations should agree to the request.' On that premise, the ACAS advice does not go far enough. It almost certainly would be directly or indirectly discriminatory to refuse such a request if there was an available place and it would not cause problems.

Employers who set aside a room for members only of specified religions would be risking a direct discrimination claim from members of other religions and, arguably, from those who are not religious but would like to be able to use a quiet room for contemplation.

Dress codes

Dress codes which have the effect of conflicting with religious requirements may constitute indirect discrimination unless they can be justified.

In *Dawkins v Department of the Environment* [1993] IRLR 284, a Rastafarian was turned down for a job as a van driver because his hair was arranged in dreadlocks. Dreadlocks are regarded by Rastafarians as representing the Lion of Judah and are essential to their belief. Mr Dawkins was informed that the employers expected their drivers to have short hair, but he indicated that he was unwilling to cut his hair. It was accepted by the employers that Mr Dawkins was refused employment because he was a Rastafarian, but his race discrimination claim was unsuccessful when the Court of Appeal held that Rastafarians are not a group defined by reference

to 'ethnic origins' and therefore not a 'racial group' within the meaning of the Race Relations Act 1976, s 3(1). Rastafarianism is listed in the ACAS Guide as one of the common religions in Britain, so a ban on dreadlocks will now be indirectly discriminatory, subject to the employer having the defence that the dress code is a proportionate means of achieving a legitimate aim.

The ACAS Guide gives several other examples. One is an organisation that states that men may not wear ponytails. 'This may indirectly disadvantage Hindu men, some of whom wear a Shika (a small knotted tuft of hair worn at the back of the head, as a symbol of their belief).' Another illustration is a dress code that requires a blouse to be tucked inside a skirt. Since this accentuates body shapes, it may conflict with a religious requirement that female followers dress particularly modestly. ACAS points out that 'if the individual is allowed to wear the blouse over the outside of the skirt it may be quite acceptable.'

Khalsa Sikhs are required to wear five religious symbols, one of which is uncut hair, which means a beard for men and hair covered by a turban.

Items of jewellery and markings are traditional within some religions of beliefs. The ACAS Guide notes that: 'In addition to a wedding ring, many Hindu women wear a necklace (Mangal Sutra) which is placed around their neck during the wedding ceremony and is therefore highly symbolic. Some may find it distressing if they are not allowed to wear it in their place of work, unless the rule was for health and safety or other justifiable reasons.'

Health and safety is the most obvious potential justification for a dress or appearance code. In a sex discrimination context, however, the courts have tended to defer more generally to management views of what is appropriate. In *Schmidt v Austicks Bookshops Ltd* [1977] IRLR 360, the EAT said that an employer is entitled to a large measure of discretion in controlling the image of his establishment. The most recent EAT decision in this area, *Department for Work and Pensions v Thompson* (27 November 2003) was a case in which men working for Jobcentre Plus were required to wear a collar and tie, whereas women were required merely to 'dress appropriately and to a similar standard'. The case is of relevance because the EAT pointed out that the employer's overarching requirement was for its staff to dress in a 'professional and businesslike way.' What the employment tribunal should have addressed was whether this 'could only be achieved for men by requiring them to wear a collar and tie.' If a level of smartness for men which equates to dressing in a professional and businesslike way could be achieved by men dressing otherwise than in a collar and tie, 'then the lack of flexibility in the dress code introduced by Jobcentre Plus would suggest that male members of staff are being treated less favourably than female members of staff because it would not have been necessary to restrict men's choice of what to wear in order to achieve the standard of smartness required.'

Similar principles might be applied to cases where clothing or appearance associated with particular religious or belief groups was concerned, although the issue is likely to be one of indirect, rather than direct, discrimination. If an employer can achieve the image required without banning dress associated with a particular religious or belief group, such a prohibition is unlikely to be regarded as 'a proportionate means of achieving a legitimate aim.'

The hijab

There is considerable current controversy over the wearing of the hijab or Islamic headscarf, which some Muslim women wear to cover their head, neck and throat (the word comes from the Arabic hajaba, meaning to hide from view). This derives from the code of modesty laid down in the Qur'an, which dictates that a Muslim woman should cover her whole body except her face.

The French Government has decided to ban the hijab from State schools, along with other 'ostensible' religious symbols such as yarmulkes and prominent crucifixes, and possibly even Sikh turbans, that 'conspicuously manifest the religious affiliation of the pupils'. Small symbols, such as small crosses, Stars of David or Muslim insignia such as little Korans will be tolerated. French President Jacques Chirac asserted that wearing a hijab was a form of proselytising, which

was inconsistent with the French principle which removes religion from all State educational institutions. There was widespread support for this across the political spectrum in France, with the French National Assembly voting by 494 votes to 36 in favour of the ban.

This has only been an issue so far in a few British schools, most notably, Icknield High in Luton, where the hijab was banned as analogous to the school's uniform policy prohibiting hats, provoking demonstrations from al-Muhajiroun, a radical Muslim group.

On the view taken in France, the hijab is a symbol of Islamic separatism and of the repression of women that is politically offensive to others. It is associated with countries in which women are denied many rights, including the freedom to work where they choose.

It is said that many girls and women are intimidated into wearing the headscarf. The French law will also cover Muslim pupils who have refused to attend history lessons for fear that they would be taught about the Jewish Holocaust, an event that anti-Semitic Islamists deny.

Others take the view that a person's chosen headcovering, whether it be a turban, a hijab, or a yarmulke, regardless of its symbolism, cannot be viewed as offensive, and that the right to choose how one dresses is fundamental to a tolerant and liberal society. In this context, it can be pointed out that schools – and workplaces – which once required women to wear skirts, have usually adapted their policies in the face of objections, sometimes from Muslims. Attacks on wearing the hijab can be regarded as essentially a manifestation of anti-Muslim prejudice and as applying a stereotype that a Muslim woman who wears a hijab is oppressed and has no choice in the matter.

Although recent publicity has concerned wearing of the hijab by students, and there is little evidence that it has become a workplace issue yet in Britain, issues may well arise under the new Regulations in the future. For a start, the Regulations cover providers of vocational training, including colleges providing such training. Moreover, cases in other European countries have involved rules laid down by employers prohibiting employees from wearing a hijab. Thus, in Denmark, in a case brought by HK, the Danish trade union confederation against Fotex, the High Court ruled against a supermarket cashier who was dismissed after she insisted on wearing a hijab after adopting a stricter form of Islam. The company said this breached its dress code, which also prohibits prominent Christian symbols as well as gaudy hair colourings and nose rings.

In *Dahlab v Switzerland* (423393/98, 15 February 2001), the European Court of Human Rights rejected a claim under Article 9 of the Convention by a Swiss primary school teacher who converted to Islam and was dismissed after she insisted on wearing an Islamic headscarf in class. The Court took the view that the interference with the applicant's right to religious freedom was justified in principle and proportionate. Noting that the applicant was teaching young pupils, the ECHR said 'it cannot be denied outright that the wearing of a headscarf might have some kind of proselytising effect, seeing that it appears to be imposed on women by a precept which is laid down in the Koran and which ... is hard to square with the principle of gender equality. It therefore appears difficult to reconcile the wearing of an Islamic headscarf with the message of tolerance, respect for others and, above all, equality and non-discrimination that all teachers in a democratic society must convey to their pupils.'

Situating a hypothetical hijab ban by an employer under the Religion or Belief Regulations, on one view, as indicated earlier in this chapter, such a prohibition could be regarded as inherently discrimination on grounds of religious belief if the correct interpretation of the law is that belief includes manifestation of a central tenet of the person's religion.

If that is not the case, then whether such a ban is direct discrimination on grounds of religion or belief will depend on how the employer treats or would treat people in similar circumstances of different religions. That is to say, the key question will be has the employer merely banned the wearing of the hijab or other Islamic manifestations, or has the employer prohibited wearing of symbols of other religions. If the employer has singled out Muslims, if the tribunal finds that the circumstances are comparable, that will be direct discrimination. However, we might expect an employer in such a case to argue that the circumstances are not comparable. For example, it might be said that the hijab is regarded as offensive by some employees as a symbol of extremism and oppression of women, whereas similar complaints were not made about other religious displays.

If, on the other hand, the employer bans all overt religious symbols from the workplace, then an issue of indirect discrimination might arise if this placed members of a particular religious group at a disadvantage.

Dietary requirements

Many religious and belief groups have particular dietary requirements. Failure by an employer to accommodate these after having received a request will present an indirect discrimination issue. The employer will then have to justify this failure to accommodate in accordance with the usual principles of indirect discrimination law, that is to say that the employer will have to show that the policy is 'a proportionate means of achieving a legitimate aim.'

Alternative meals in the canteen are the most obvious example. Most employers will already provide a vegetarian alternative, but there may also be requests for halal or kosher meals. Whether a policy of not providing such meals, if requested to do so, would be lawful will depend on considerations such as the cost and inconvenience to the employer of arranging for such an alternative.

ACAS points out that 'if staff bring food into the workplace they may need to store and heat food separately from other food, for example Muslims will wish to ensure their food is not in contact with pork (or anything that may have been in contact with pork, such as cloths and sponges).'

Non-alcoholic drinks and vegetarian food options should be provided at events outside normal working hours.

Working hours, time off and holidays

If an employer deals with requests for prayer breaks in a different way as between members of different religious groups in similar circumstances, this would constitute direct discrimination.

The DTI explanatory notes give as an example of possible indirect discrimination an employer who refuses work breaks for all his employees on shift work between 6 am and 9 am, pointing out that a Muslim employee's faith requires them to take breaks from work to pray at certain times of the day. It would then be for the employer to justify the practice of refusing all work breaks. The DTI points out that this could be due to factors such as lack of space, the expense of providing facilities, or the incompatibility of prayer breaks with the nature of the work. 'It would then be a question of whether the refusal of *all* breaks could be considered proportionate to that aim. The nature of the work may demonstrate an essential requirement for all staff to be working throughout that whole period. But if other staff can cover a brief absence, or staff taking a short break can make up later for any time lost, that would suggest the refusal is not proportionate to the aim.'

Time off for prayers is especially important for Muslims during the winter, when three of the five prayer times fall within the normal working day.

Where employees are fasting for religious reasons, such as Muslims during Ramadan, their concentration may be affected and they may require early release for health and safety reasons.

As part of their sabbath observance, some religions do not allow employees to work at certain times. For example, observant orthodox Jews cannot work on Friday evening or Saturdays. An employer who did not adjust the hours of such an employee would have to be prepared to justify this indirect discrimination. One way of dealing with such issues is to become more flexible about working hours generally. Croydon London Borough Council, for example, is reported (*People Management*, 4 December 2003) as having moved from flexitime to a 'worksmart' system whereby staff do not have to work a core number of hours but can arrange job shares or work from home. This will make it easier for Muslims, for example, not to work on Friday.

Sabbath working

Practising Christians who wish to keep Sunday holy have often been obliged to work, since until now the only groups who have enjoyed legal protection as regards being required to work on Sunday are shop workers and betting shop employees.

A Sunday working requirement is a typical indirect discrimination case that is likely to be raised under the new Regulations. This will disadvantage workers holding the belief that the sabbath is a day of rest, and the question will be whether the employer is insisting on Sunday working because of a legitimate aim and, more importantly, whether it is proportionate in the particular case. That means, for example, whether the employer can meet its staff needs for Sunday working by calling for volunteers rather than making it compulsory.

An unsuccessful attempt was made in *Stedman v United Kingdom* (1987) 23 EHRR CD 168 to use Article 9 of the European Convention to challenge a Sunday working requirement. The European Commission on Human Rights took the narrow view that the employee's rights under the Convention were not infringed because she could seek alternative employment that would allow her to observe the Sabbath. It is unlikely that British tribunals and courts will adopt the same approach in interpreting the Regulations.

There is a more directly relevant case on Sunday working from the Northern Ireland religious discrimination jurisdiction. In *Kennedy v Gallaher Ltd*, the employers decided to change their working pattern, following an increase in demand, so as to incorporate six-day working for the factory. They were indifferent as to whether Saturday or Sunday would be the rest day. The trade unions balloted the workforce, who voted by a two to one majority to have Saturday off. Mary Kennedy refused to work

Sundays on grounds of her religious belief. This meant that she could not be employed on rotating shifts, thereby resulting in a loss of pay. She claimed that this was indirectly discriminatory. The Fair Employment Tribunal accepted that the Sunday working requirement had an adverse impact on those with the same belief as Mrs Kennedy, but held that the employers had justified the requirement. The Tribunal concluded that the discriminatory effect of the discrimination was outweighed by the reasonable needs of the employer.

The case then went to the Northern Ireland Court of Appeal (21 October 1993), who dismissed the appeal. It held that in measuring the reasonable needs of the employer, 'significant weight should be given to the fact that the vast majority of the workforce suffer no detriment by reason of the requirement.' It took the view that the quantitative effect of the detriment suffered was a material consideration. Thus, it did not accept that 'once a minority of the workforce, no matter how small, has been shown to have suffered indirect religious discrimination that in itself must prevail in the balancing exercise in the test of justifiability.' Instead, the Northern Ireland Court of Appeal took the view that the reasonable needs of the employer outweighed the discriminatory effect of the requirement because the employers had little alternative but to reflect the preference shown of the vast majority of its workforce to work on Saturdays rather than Sundays. The Court of Appeal said that for the employers to impose on the workforce a work week not of their declared choice and to act against the decision of a joint working party would not have conformed to the standards of reasonable consultation, and a special arrangement with the employee would have been contrary to the decision of the representative working party against one-off arrangements.

In Great Britain, those dismissed for refusing to work Sundays on religious grounds have attempted to use unfair dismissal law, buttressed more recently by human rights principles. Copsey v WBB Devon Clays, a case brought by an evangelical Christian with the support of the Keep Sunday Special campaign is the latest example of this. In a decision handed down in February 2004, the EAT rejected an appeal dismissing Mr Copsey's unfair dismissal claim. The employers had introduced a seven-day shift system after a surge in demand, following consultation with the unions and with the support of a majority of the employees. It is inevitable that similar cases will now be brought directly under the Religion or Belief Regulations.

Note that if an employer decides to use volunteers for Sunday and pays a premium rate for this, the DTI explanatory notes flag up a potential problem: 'Such arrangements may constitute indirect discrimination if they are not justified, because they may disadvantage those employees whose faith recognises a day of rest other than Sunday. However, in many cases the employer may be able to justify such arrangements by reference to market forces, which require her to pay those rates for Sundays (but not other days) in order to attract sufficient staff to work on Sundays.'

Similar considerations in respect of Sunday working arise as regards working on a different day of the week, such as Friday or Saturday, which an employee treats as the sabbath as a result of their religious beliefs.

Time off for holidays

Where an employer operates a holiday system involving an annual shutdown or closures for other specific periods and requires all staff to take annual holiday at that time, this create difficulties if it prevents individuals from taking annual leave at times of special religious significance to them.

An indirect discrimination issue which is frequently raised is whether it is justifiable to require non-Christian employees to take a day of holiday on Christmas Day, in circumstances where those employees are required to use up their holiday entitlement for religious festivals at other times of the year. The DTI explanatory notes take the position that 'in most cases the requirement could be justified on the basis that Christmas Day is a holiday which is widely recognised throughout Britain, on which very few business are open for trade; and furthermore, most employees (regardless of their faith) might expect to have the day as a holiday, thus making it difficult for an employer to find a sufficient number of employees to work on Christmas Day. In those circumstances, the vast majority of employers would be justified in requiring their employees to take time off on Christmas Day so that the business can close down.'

But what if most employees in the business want to have Eid off and ask that the firm shut down for that holiday? That might raise some interesting issues as to justification if the request is refused. Transport for London is reported to be considering replacing bank holidays with a number of 'floating days' which will allow non-Christians to work through Christmas and Easter (*People Management*, 4 December 2003).

Employers who seek to accommodate employees by allowing them additional time off with pay to observe their own holidays may be vulnerable to a claim of direct discrimination from employees of a different religion or no religion. The DTI gives this as an example: 'if an employer gives a Jewish employee an extra day of paid holiday in order to mark a religious festival, this would be direct discrimination against employees who are atheist or follow other faiths, because they are treated less favourably on grounds of their religious beliefs. If the Jewish employee were required to use one day of his existing holiday entitlement to mark the festival, there would be no direct discrimination against other employees.' What if an employer allows a Muslim employee to work over Christmas but pays them double time to do so, does this mean that a Christian employee who works over Ramadan but receives no extra payment can claim that they are being discriminated against? This might not succeed if the employer in such a case was able to argue that the reason for the difference in payment was not religion but was instead staff shortages over the Christmas period as compared with Ramadan.

Chapter 9

Discrimination on grounds of sexual orientation

The Employment Equality (Sexual Orientation) Regulations 2003, which came into force on 1 December 2003, represent the culmination of a long legal struggle by lesbians and gay men to secure a remedy against discrimination in the workplace.

Surveys suggest a substantial proportion of lesbians and gay men consider that they have been discriminated against at work. Yet attempts to use EU equal pay law and sex discrimination law to provide a remedy met with failure. Those attempts to bootstrap sexual orientation rights on to sex discrimination law are no longer necessary. As a result of the Framework Employment Directive and the 2003 Regulations, discrimination at work on grounds of sexual orientation is unlawful in and of itself.

Like the Religion or Belief Regulations, the general structure of the Employment Equality (Sexual Orientation) Regulations 2003 is also directly parallel to the Sex Discrimination and Race Relations Acts. Direct and indirect discrimination in employment on grounds of sexual orientation, by way of victimisation or by way of harassment is prohibited. The Regulations extend to discrimination against contract workers and by qualifications bodies. Employers are made legally liable for discrimination by their employees and enforcement proceedings can be brought in an employment tribunal.

The Government's Regulatory Impact Analysis estimates that there are between 1.3 and 1.9 million lesbians, gay men and bisexuals in employment who will be covered by the new Regulations. It also estimates that in the region of 1,000 new cases will be brought each year under the Regulations.

Meaning of 'sexual orientation'

The Framework Employment Directive contains no definition of 'sexual orientation'. The definition adopted in the Regulations avoids the term 'homosexual'. Instead, the definition reads:

> '"sexual orientation" means an orientation towards—
> (a) persons of the same sex,
> (b) persons of the opposite sex, or
> (c) persons of the same sex and of the opposite sex.'

As with religion, the intention here is to draw a distinction between a person's 'orientation', which is protected, and manifestations of their orientation or behaviour, which may not be protected. The DTI explanatory notes state unequivocally: 'The definition does not include sexual practices or sexual conduct. As the definition says, a sexual orientation is simply

an orientation towards persons of the same sex, the opposite sex, or both sexes.' The explanatory memorandum issued to accompany the Regulations when they were laid before Parliament reveals the underlying thinking. It says that the definition 'does not extend to sexual practices and preferences (eg sado-masochism and paedophilia).' This is not really surprising. The Government would not relish tabloid newspaper headlines about discrimination laws protecting people with unusual sexual practices. However, it is doubtful whether 'paedophilia' can be categorised as a sexual 'orientation' under any standard.

It might have been thought that when the Framework Employment Directive declares that discrimination on grounds of 'sexual orientation' must be prohibited, that this could be regarded as encompassing a person's orientation towards bondage or sexual domination, and not merely whether they are gay or bisexual or straight. It is clear that the Religion or Belief Regulations (see Chapter 9) are not limited to protecting against discrimination on grounds of belonging to a religion, they also extend to discrimination on grounds of adherence to a sect of that religion. A man who is discriminated against, for example, because he wears the hat, long coat and beard associated with Chassidic Jews would appear to be entitled to protection on that ground. Why does not the same apply to, for example, a gay man whose orientation is towards the world of leather, or a straight woman who is sexually a submissive?

However, that does not seem to be the Government's view of what is protected by the Directive or the Regulations. Instead, the same distinction is drawn as with religion or belief, between sexual orientation itself and manifestations of sexual orientation.

The recent decision of the EAT in *Pay v Lancashire Probation Service* [2004] IRLR 129 provides a useful vehicle to consider the effect of this limitation. The case involved an unfair dismissal complaint by a probation officer working with sex offenders who was dismissed after his employers discovered that he was involved in activities which included performing in fetish clubs and merchandising BDSM products. The main issue is whether dismissal on this ground constituted an infringement of the employee's rights under the European Convention on Human Rights to respect for his private life and to freedom of expression. The EAT held that Mr Pay's right to freedom of expression had been engaged, although the interference with that right was justified. Judge McMullen's decision draws attention to the interpretive obligation on tribunals and courts deriving from the Human Rights Act 1998, s 3(1) which provides that 'so far as it is possible to do so, primary legislation and subordinate legislation must be read and given effect in a way which is compatible with the Convention rights.' In the context of *Pay*, which was an unfair dismissal case, this leads the EAT to hold that an employer – or at least a public authority employer – will not act reasonably under the Employment Rights Act 1996, s 98(4) if it violates an employee's Convention rights. Accordingly, the EAT says, a tribunal should interpret the words 'reasonably or unreasonably' in the test of unfair dismissal as including 'having regard to the applicant's Convention rights'.

If we take that as a general principle and apply it to the new Regulations, it would mean that the right not to be discriminated against on grounds of 'sexual orientation' would be interpreted as including 'having regard to the applicant's Convention rights'. Would that entail giving a broader reading to the concept of 'sexual orientation' than that envisaged by the DTI, so as to encompass an applicant's freedom to express their sexual orientation by manifesting it?

Manifestations of sexual orientation

The importance of this point becomes clear when we consider the implications of the DTI's position that discrimination on grounds of manifestations of sexual orientation is not necessarily discrimination on grounds of sexual orientation, in the same way that discrimination on grounds of manifesting religious belief is not necessarily discrimination on grounds of religion or belief. It is true that the DTI explanatory notes refer to 'sexual practices or sexual conduct', which suggests a sexual act rather than

sexual behaviour generally, but there is no principled distinction between the two. If orientation 'is simply an orientation', it does not necessarily cover behaviour of any kind which manifests that orientation.

Suppose an employer says 'we are happy to employ lesbians, but we want all our female employees to look feminine because that is what the customers like.' On the DTI's analysis, if a stereotypically butch lesbian is rejected because, in the employer's view, she appears too 'mannish', that would not be direct discrimination on grounds of sexual orientation as such, if the employers applied the same standard to all women and would reject a heterosexual woman who did not conform to their standard either. It would only be discriminatory if it could be shown to be unjustifiable indirect discrimination against people with an orientation towards the same sex.

Direct discrimination

The definition of direct discrimination in respect of sexual orientation provides:

> 'For the purposes of these Regulations, a person ("A") discriminates against another person ("B") if—
> (a) on grounds of sexual orientation, A treats B less favourably than he treats or would treat other persons...'

The general principle, therefore, is that in most cases a lesbian or gay man seeking to establish direct discrimination will have to compare their treatment to an actual or hypothetical person of a different sexual orientation. Thus:

- if a business arranges work-related marketing functions at which employees and clients bring their partners, it would be direct discrimination to discourage a lesbian or gay employee from bringing their partner;
- if two women are disciplined for holding hands in front of the customers, that will be discriminatory if a man and a woman would not have been so disciplined. The employer's only defence would be that any employees holding

hands would be disciplined in the same way, regardless of their sexual orientation.

- if a gay man is asked not to bring his male partner to a Christmas dinner because it would embarrass the wives, he will be able to show direct discrimination if a similar request would not have been made to him if he had a female partner.
- if a woman is dismissed because the employer discovers that she is having a relationship with a work colleague of the same sex, that will be direct discrimination if the employer would not have dismissed a worker discovered to be in a relationship with a colleague of the opposite sex.

Unlike the comparable provisions in respect of religious discrimination, nothing has been added to the definition that specifies that it is only the claimant's sexual orientation that is relevant. Accordingly, on the principle that Parliament must have intended to distinguish between the two Regulations in this respect, the definition of direct discrimination in these Regulations must be taken as covering discrimination by a person because of their own sexual orientation. For example, the definition would encompass harassment of another man by A, regardless of the sexual orientation of the man harassed.

In order to avoid direct discrimination on grounds of sexual orientation, employers will need to monitor their policies and practices and eliminate anything which directly treats lesbians, gay men and bisexuals less favourably than heterosexuals. If an employer offers bereavement leave to heterosexuals who are married or in a long-term relationship, it would be directly discriminatory not to offer the same leave to a gay person in a similar relationship.

Perceived discrimination and discrimination by association

Because the definition of direct discrimination is phrased in terms of 'on grounds of sexual orientation' rather than on grounds of 'his' or 'her' sexual orientation, it is unlawful to discriminate on grounds of a perception about someone's sexual orientation, even if that perception is factually inaccurate. Indeed,

if an applicant can establish that the ground for the treatment was their perceived sexual orientation, their claim will succeed regardless of what their actual sexual orientation was.

This will cover someone discriminated against because they are thought to 'look gay', 'dress gay', or 'act gay'. For example, on being shown out of an interview room, a woman overhears one of the interviewers saying 'we can't possibly have her, she looks so butch, she would never fit in.' This assumption about her sexual orientation would be valid grounds for a complaint whether or not the woman's sexual orientation was lesbian. If the case went to a tribunal, it would not be necessary for the woman to disclose her sexual orientation if she chose not to.

Similarly, if someone is harassed at work because they have gay friends with whom they socialise, this will be sexual orientation regardless of the actual sexual orientation of the person harassed and even though their sexual orientation might be the same as that of the harasser. Likewise, if someone, whatever their sexual orientation, is discriminated against or harassed because they live with someone who is HIV-positive.

Harassment

The freestanding prohibition of harassment on grounds of sexual orientation is one of the areas of the new Regulations likely to have the most impact. A survey carried out by Stonewall in 1993 ('Less Equal than Others') found that 48% of lesbians, gay men and bisexuals taking part said that they had been harassed at work.

Someone who is harassed because of their sexual orientation no longer has to use the Sex Discrimination Act to try to show that someone of the same sexual orientation but a different gender would have been treated more favourably. It will be sufficient for them to establish that someone of a different sexual orientation would not have been harassed.

In Chapter 2 on harassment, we pointed out that the definition of harassment covers conduct that either has the effect of violating the employee's dignity or of creating a hostile working environment for them. This does not require that the conduct must be directed at the employee concerned. Thus, an atmosphere in which homophobic jokes and slurs abounded could create an offensive working environment for a gay or lesbian employee even if they were not specifically directed at the employee. The DTI explanatory notes give this example: 'if jokes which are degrading to lesbians are emailed by employees to one another, this would be harassment if it violates the dignity of a lesbian employee or creates a degrading or humiliating environment for her.'

The fact that many lesbians and gay men are not 'out' at work poses particular problems in this regard both for themselves and for employers. From their own standpoint, if their sexual orientation is not known, they are more likely to be subjected to unwitting homophobic harassment. Yet in order to get the harassment to stop, by complaining they may risk 'outing' themselves.

From an employer's perspective, the organisation is less likely to be aware of the sexual orientation of those subjected to homophobic harassment than of their sex or race or even disability. Such lack of knowledge, however, will not relieve an employer of responsibility for the harassment, since ordinary principles of legal liability apply. As reg 22(1) puts it: 'Anything done by a person in the course of his employment shall be treated for the purposes of these Regulations as done by his employer as well as by him, whether or not it was done with the employer's knowledge or approval.' The obvious practical implication is that homophobic remarks, like racist comments and religious slurs, should never be regarded as acceptable workplace behaviour.

Treating employees with dignity

Much has been made of the potential conflict between the views of members of some religions about homosexuality and the rights of lesbians, bisexuals and gay men at work. If handled correctly, this is likely to be a conflict which is more illusory than real. The new protection against being subjected

to harassment embodies the principle that every employee has a right to be treated with dignity and respect at work. The expression of homophobic views infringes such a right and it does not matter at all whether the motivation for those views is religious principle or simply bigotry. It is highly improbable that the tribunals will regard it as discrimination on grounds of religion or belief to discipline an employee who contravenes the employer's dignity policy by expressing homophobic views. The reverse should apply as well. Some lesbians and gay men find fundamentalist religious views offensive and may wish to make that clear. If that takes in the workplace, it is also likely to be inconsistent with a dignity policy.

Note that employers are potentially legally liable for harassment on grounds of sexual orientation whether the recipients of the harassment are their own employees or are temporary workers sent by an employment agency. Temporary workers are contract workers and have parallel rights as against the client or 'principal'. Therefore, an employer should have no lower standards as regards protecting the dignity of temporary workers and their working environment from harassment on grounds of sexual orientation than they do for their own permanent employees.

Other detrimental treatment

Regulation 6(2)(b) provides that it is unlawful for an employer to discriminate against an employee on grounds of their sexual orientation by 'subjecting them to a detriment'. We pointed out earlier in this book that both the Sexual Orientation Regulations and the Religion or Belief Regulations state that for the purposes of the Regulations, a '"detriment" does not include harassment within the meaning of reg 5.' This means that which is harassment cannot also be discrimination by way of a detriment, though the prudent applicant will try to run both claims at the same time.

Because of the way the definition is framed, a tribunal will first have to determine whether the conduct complained of is harassment, and then, if it is not, whether it is a detriment. Regardless of where the line between the harassment and detriment is drawn, however, certain treatment which is not harassive itself in nature may fall to be regarded as detrimental treatment.

Most large employers have taken steps to provide a supportive working environment for women, minority ethnic people and employees who are disabled. As a general principle, if an employer refuses to extend their policies and procedures in this regard to lesbians, gay men and bisexuals, they could be vulnerable to a detrimental treatment claim.

Thus, if an employer has a bullying and harassment policy but refuses to include harassment based on sexual orientation within the scope of the policy, that is likely to be regarded as detrimental treatment on grounds of sexual orientation. This may be the case even where the employer is not legally liable for the harassment itself, as with harassment of teachers by pupils or employees by customers.

The extent to which the employer provides a welcoming environment for people regardless of their sexual orientation, making it safe for them to come out is an issue of considerable importance for lesbians and gay men. Employee networks – forums for staff who share one or more aspects of their identity – have become increasingly popular and they are often funded and promoted by employers. Employee networks for women and for black staff have been operating in many large public, private and voluntary sector organisations for some time.

It would be good practice for an employer to provide assistance in establishing a network for lesbians, gay men and bisexual (LGB) employees, since that will demonstrate the organisation's commitment to workplace diversity. Stonewall's Guidelines for employers points out that an LGB employee network can challenge the invisibility of LGB staff and issues; give LGB staff a forum for sharing experiences; allow organisations to tap into the specific experience and knowledge of LGB staff; and help LGB staff to come out and other employees to appreciate the diversity of the organisation.

But the issue is not simply one of good practice. If an employer is asked by gay staff for help and facilities in establishing an employee network and rejects the request, this is likely to be regarded as subjecting lesbians and gay men to a detriment contrary to the Regulations if the inference can be drawn that the employer would have agreed to the request were it not in connection with facilities for gay staff. This will be especially the case where the employer has assisted in creating other networks. Similar considerations apply to requests for rooms for meetings or to establish a help line, for example.

The ACAS Guide points out that 'organisations and their staff should not assume that everyone is heterosexual. If organisations offer the opportunity for social gatherings which extend to the partners of staff, care should be taken with the wording of invitations, posters, etc to ensure inclusion of those with same sex partners. Where opposite sex partners are invited, the exclusion of same sex partners is hurtful and may constitute discrimination.' Similarly, social events involving partners and children should be made equally open to same sex partners and their children.

The US Human Rights Campaign Foundation produces a Corporate Equality Index that rates large businesses in America on how they treat their gay, lesbian, bisexual and transgender employees. The five points relating to employment are instructive:

'1. Has a written non-discrimination policy covering sexual orientation in its employee handbook or manual.

2. Has a written non-discrimination policy covering gender identity and/or expression in its employee handbook or manual.

3. Offers health insurance coverage to employees' same-sex domestic partners.

4. Officially recognises and supports a lesbian, gay, bisexual and transgender employee resource group or council or has a company policy that gives employee groups equal standing regardless of sexual orientation and gender identity.

5. Offers diversity training that includes sexual orientation and/or gender expression in the workplace.'

Readers might be interested that 13 companies received perfect scores in 2002: Aetna Inc, AMR Corp/American Airlines, Apple Computer Inc, Avaya Inc, Eastman Kodak Co, Intel Corp, J P Morgan Chase & Co, Lucent Technologies Inc, NCR Corp, Nike Inc, Replacements Ltd, Worldspan LP, and Xerox Corp.

Genuine occupational requirement

The Regulations allow an employer to discriminate on grounds of sexual orientation in respect of recruitment, promotion, transfer, training or dismissal in certain circumstances. These are specified in reg 7(2) and (3). Regulation 7(2) allows discrimination on grounds of sexual orientation if a three-stage test is satisfied:

'where, having regard to the nature of the employment or the context in which it is carried out –
(a) being of a particular sexual orientation is a genuine and determining occupational requirement;
(b) it is proportionate to apply that requirement in the particular case; and
(c) either –
(i) the person to whom the requirement is applied does not meet it, or
(ii) the employer is not satisfied, and in all the circumstances it is reasonable for him not to be satisfied,
and this paragraph applies whether or not the employment is for purposes of an organised religion.'

Regulation 7(2) does not adopt all the language of the Directive and has been criticised for failing to transpose the Directive correctly. Article 4(2) of the Directive stipulates that a genuine and determining occupational requirement can justify discrimination only where 'the objective is legitimate and the requirement is proportionate.' Regulation 7(2) omits the requirements both of legitimacy and proportionality.

Be that as it may, outside the context of a religious or counselling environment, it is difficult to think of posts where a sexual orientation GOR might apply. The DTI suggests that 'it is very rare indeed that being of a particular sexual orientation is a genuine occupational requirement for a job under reg 7(2).' According to the DTI, 'in the vast majority of jobs, a person's sexual orientation has no bearing on whether or not they can carry out the job in question. However, a GOR may be justified in a small number of cases.' The following example is then given: 'it may be possible to establish a GOR to be gay or lesbian, having regard to the context of the work, for persons in a position of leadership in, or representing the public face of, an organisation concerned with advising gay men and lesbians about their rights, or promoting those rights. In those circumstances there may be an issue of credibility which makes it a GOR for the person to be gay or lesbian in order to perform the functions of the post. On the other hand, for posts in the organisation which simply involve advising gays and lesbians about their legal rights, no GOR would apply because it is not essential to be gay or lesbian in order to offer good legal advice to gays and lesbians. The mere fact that the people receiving the advice might prefer to deal with a gay or lesbian adviser does not make it a GOR for the job.'

This example is convincing. Its counterpart in a religious discrimination context would be a requirement that the Pope be a Catholic! It is rather more persuasive than the GOR example used by the DTI, discussed in the chapter on religion or belief discrimination, of the advisor in a Christian support group.

It is fundamental that merely because clients or customers might prefer to deal with someone of a particular sexual orientation does not make that a GOR. Were that not the case, pandering to customer or client preference would drive a coach and horses through discrimination legislation.

Perceived failure to meet the GOR

Regulation 7(2)(c) provides that the genuine occupational requirement exception can apply either where the employee or job applicant does not meet the requirement, or where 'the employer is not satisfied, and in all the circumstances it is reasonable for him not to be satisfied' that the employee or applicant meets the requirement.

The burden of proof is on the employer to establish that all the elements of a GOR are met, and therefore it is for the employer, if necessary, to establish, for example, that an applicant was gay or that it was reasonable for him not to be satisfied that their orientation was not 'to members of the opposite sex', to use the language of the Regulations.

There is no obligation on a job applicant (or an employee) to disclose their sexual orientation. If the employer was seeking to recruit for a job to which it believed that a GOR applied which would rule out a gay man or lesbian, the employer would have to demonstrate that he was 'not satisfied' that the applicant was not gay, and that it was 'reasonable' for him to be satisfied that the applicant was gay.

When will it be reasonable for this assumption to be made about someone's sexual orientation? In 'The Outing' episode of *Seinfeld*, Jerry is concerned that some people might think that he is gay because 'I'm single, I'm thin and I'm neat.' Elaine adds 'And you get along with women.' Comedy becomes reality under the Sexual Orientation Regulations. Could an employer assume that because an applicant lives with someone of the same sex that they have an orientation towards persons of that sex? Is personal appearance sufficient? Clothing? Mannerisms? Perhaps employers will use psychometric tests that will weed out lesbians and gay men?

This is one of the aspects of the Regulations being challenged by way of an application for judicial review brought by Amicus and Unison (*Amicus – MSF section v Secretary of State for Trade and Industry*) on grounds that it goes beyond the permissible scope of the Framework Employment Directive and as contravening Articles 8 and 14 of the European Convention on Human Rights. The main arguments are that the GOR does not use the language of the Directive in that it does not include any provision that the discriminatory requirement must meet some 'legitimate objective', and that it allows an employer

to rely on a GOR even where a person has the sexual orientation required for the post, if the employer is not satisfied, and in all the circumstances it is reasonable for him not to be satisfied, that that person meets the GOR. The case was scheduled for a High Court hearing on 17-19 March 2004.

The wording of the Regulations on perceived sexual orientation is defended by the DTI on the basis that if an employer could rely on the GOR exception only where he could prove that the job applicant was in fact unable to meet the GOR, the employer might feel compelled to engage in intrusive questioning and investigation in order to ascertain the actual sexual orientation of a job applicant.

Nevertheless, the mind boggles as to the evidence that might be regarded as probative of this point and at the prospect of the judges deciding when it is reasonable for an employer to be satisfied that someone is lesbian or gay.

Organised religion GOR

Regulation 7(3) provides a much more controversial broader genuine occupational requirement exception in relation to employment for the purposes of an organised religion. It also lays down a three-stage test. The GOR applies where –

'(a) the employment is for the purposes of an organised religion;
(b) the employer applies a requirement related to sexual orientation –
(i) so as to comply with the doctrines of the religion or
(ii) because of the nature of the employment and the context
in which it is carried out, so as to avoid conflicting with the strongly held religious convictions of a significant number of the religion's followers; and
(c) either –
(i) the person to whom the requirement is applied does not meet it, or
(ii) the employer is not satisfied, and in all the circumstances it is reasonable for him not to be satisfied, that that person meets it.'

The key practical issue is the scope of this exclusion: does it give faith-based schools and care homes the right to exclude lesbian, gay and bisexual employees? Does it go even further and mean that employers will be able to prevent lesbian, gay and bisexual people from working for any school, voluntary organisation, charity or private company with a religious ethos? The Government's view, as noted below, is that this is not what was intended, and that the scope of the exclusion is much more narrow. However, it is by no means clear that an ethos-based organisation which seeks to exclude lesbian and gay employees could not bring itself within the terms of the GOR by using appropriate drafting for contracts of employment, mission statements, trust deeds etc.

It is to be noted that there is a direct parallel to this part of reg 7(3) in the Sex Discrimination Act 1975, s 19 which provides: 'Nothing in this Part applies to employment for the purposes of an organised religion where the employment is limited to one sex so as to comply with the doctrines of the religion or avoid offending the religious susceptibilities of a significant number of its followers.' Although it has been on the statute books for nearly 30 years, this does not seem to have generated a great deal of controversy in practice.

Regulation 7(3) is also being challenged in the judicial review case. It is argued by the applicants that the criteria set out bear little relation to Article 4(1) of the Directive in that it is not necessary for the employer to show that being of a particular sexual orientation is 'genuine', or that it is 'determining', or that there is an objective which is 'legitimate', or that the requirement is 'proportionate'. Moreover, Article 4(2) of the Directive, having set out the terms on which a genuine occupational requirement on grounds of religion or belief is permissible, then states that this is subject to the proviso that: 'This difference of treatment … should not justify discrimination on another ground.'

The application for judicial review follows a report from the Parliamentary Joint Committee on Statutory Instruments casting doubt on whether the scope of this Regulation went further than permitted by the Directive. In their 21st report (13 June 2003), having heard evidence from DTI officials, the Committee expressed concern that reg 7(3) 'might permit difference of treatment based on a characteristic related to sexual orientation where the characteristic could not be said to be a "genuine and determining occupational requirement" which was proportionate, as envisaged by the Directive.'

This was followed by a lengthy debate in the House of Lords on 17 June 2003 on a motion by Lord Lester of Herne Hill to withdraw the Regulations, which was replied to on behalf of the Government by Lord Sainsbury. Lord Sainsbury's remarks explaining the rationale behind reg 7(3) may be taken into account where a court or tribunal regards the language of the Regulations as ambiguous, in accordance with the principle laid down in *Pepper v Hart.*

According to Lord Sainsbury,

> 'when drafting reg 7(3), we had in mind a very narrow range of employment: ministers of religion, plus a small number of posts outside the clergy, including those who exist to promote and represent religion … .It is quite clear that reg 7(3) does not apply to all jobs in a particular type of organisation. On the contrary, employers must be prepared to justify any requirement related to sexual orientation on a case-by-case basis. The rule only applies to employment which is for the purposes of "organised religion", not religious organisations. There is a clear distinction in meaning between the two. A religious organisation could be any organisation with an ethos based on religion or belief. However, employment for the purposes of an organised religion clearly means a job, such as a minister of religion, involving work for a church, synagogue or mosque.'

The explanatory notes produced by the DTI subsequently confirm this view and emphasise that the words 'employment for the purposes of an organised religion' mean that 'the employee is working for an organised religion. This formulation 'for the purposes of an organised religion' is thus narrower than the comparable provisions in reg 7(3) of the Religion or Belief Regulations, which refer to organisations with an 'ethos based on religion or belief'. According to the DTI, the GOR applies to a limited range of employment including members of the clergy or other ministers of religion, and also 'other staff working for an organised religion. They may work in a local body or place of worship such as a church, temple, or mosque, or in a body which coordinates the work of such bodies or places of worship throughout the country. For example, this may include: a General Secretary, official spokesperson, typists, support staff, cleaners' (though only if the other criteria in reg 7(3) are met).

Lord Sainsbury told Parliament that 'a care home run by a religious foundation may qualify as a religious organisation ... but I believe it would be very difficult under these Regulations to show that the job of a nurse in a care home exists, "for the purposes of an organised religion". I would say exactly the same in relation to a teacher at a faith school. Such jobs exist for the purposes of health care and education.' The DTI's explanatory notes also suggest that the scope of reg 7(3):

> 'would not generally apply in relation to a care home or a school with a religious ethos because the employment is for the purposes of a home providing healthcare, or a school providing education; the employees do not work for an organised religion. Only in exceptional circumstances might it be the case that an organised religion runs such an organisation (rather than simply having a representative on a board of management, or contributing to funding), such that employment there was for purposes of the religion.'

How accurate this depiction is remains to be seen. To take schools as an illustration, there certainly are schools in Britain which are directly run by organised religions and there are other institutions with a religious ethos which may wish to argue that their main aim is to provide a spiritual education, so that teachers are employed 'for the purposes of an organised religion'.

Requirement related to sexual orientation

The reason why it is so significant whether or not the scope of the organised religion GOR is narrow

is that the remainder of the GOR in reg 7(3) is much broader than the ordinary GOR in reg 7(2). Whereas reg 7(2) applies where 'being of a particular sexual orientation is a genuine and determining occupational qualification', reg 7(3) allows the organised religion employer to apply 'a requirement related to sexual orientation'. The DTI's explanatory notes give as an illustration: 'a requirement not to engage in sex with a same-sex partner would be a requirement related to sexual orientation, which would be covered by reg 7(3) but not reg 7(2).'

Religious doctrine and convictions

An employer can rely on the exception if it applies a requirement related to sexual orientation 'so as to comply with the doctrines of the religion' or 'because of the nature of the employment and the context in which it is carried out, so as to avoid conflicting with the strongly held religious convictions of a significant number of the religion's followers.'

The 'doctrines' test means that an employer must show that the religion's doctrines entail a requirement related to sexual orientation to be applied, ie that there would be a violation or breach of the doctrines of the religion if a person who did not comply with the requirement was employed. The DTI suggests that 'doctrine must represent the established teachings of a religion which is authoritative, commanding a wide, if not universal, acceptance within the religion' and that :

> 'it is unlikely that this element of reg 7(3) will be applicable in most cases of employment for purposes of an organised religion. Few religious doctrines have anything to say about heterosexuals, bisexuals, gay men or lesbians which necessitates the application of a requirement related to sexual orientation to those working for the religion. Where there are such doctrines, they are likely to apply to ministers of religion, rather than to other employees whose work is not of a spiritual nature (eg cleaners).'

Much of the commentary on this GOR presupposes that the worker concerned will be unacceptable to the organised religion because they are lesbian, gay or bisexual. However, the wording of reg 7(3), unlike reg 7(2) does not refer to 'being of a particular sexual orientation'. Instead, it allows the organised religion employer to apply 'a requirement related to sexual orientation'. Arguably, this difference in wording might allow discrimination against a cleric who had a sympathetic attitude to gay people and/or their role in the church.

Regulation 7(3)(b)(ii) allows an employer to apply a GOR because of the 'nature of the employment and the context in which it is carried out, so as to avoid conflicting with the strongly held religious convictions of a significant number of the religion's followers'. Note that the requisite causation must be established: that is to say, the GOR must be applied because of the particular nature and context of the work for an organised religion. So far as 'the strongly held religious convictions of a significant number of the religion's followers' is concerned, the DTI explanatory notes take the view that this 'may be a significant number of followers in a local context, or a regional, national or international context.' A 'significant number' is seen as meaning a 'substantial' number, but not a majority of followers. No indication is given as to what evidence a tribunal is to use to assess whether an opinion is 'strongly held'. But the DTI concludes: 'In practice, there will be very few cases under reg 7(3)(b)(ii) where a requirement for a job related to sexual orientation will be required by *both* the convictions of followers *and* the nature and context of the work.'

Overseas employment

The Sexual Orientation Regulations contain the same definition of employment in Great Britain as the Religion or Belief Regulations: if the employee works wholly outside Great Britain, the work will still be covered provided it is undertaken for the purposes of the employer's establishment in Great Britain, and the employee is (or was) ordinarily resident in Great Britain at the time of recruitment or at some time during the employment or contract work.

This will confer rights on British employees temporarily posted to other parts of the world. This

is going to present some very difficult problems for British employers who operate in Muslim countries observing a conservative form of Sharia law. Take the case of Saudi Arabia. Here is a country that prohibits public non-Muslim religious activities. Those wearing religious symbols of any kind in public risk confrontation with the religious police. As for homosexual acts, they are illegal, and subject to a maximum penalty of death. How will British employers operating in Saudi manage to reconcile this with their new discrimination law obligations?

Indirect discrimination

The definition of indirect discrimination and the general principles relating to its proof were discussed in the first part of this book.

One of the issues which may complicate potential cases of indirect discrimination on grounds of sexual orientation is the inevitable absence for the foreseeable future of accurate statistics in a particular workforce of the sexual orientation of employees. This is why it is especially significant that the Regulations refer to a provision, criterion or practice which puts or 'would put' a group at a disadvantage, thereby allowing proof of the impact of a practice on people of a particular sexual orientation without detailed statistical evidence relating to the employer in question.

Terms and conditions

The Regulations require changes to schemes that allow survivor benefits to unmarried opposite sex partners, but not to same-sex partners. The Government's Regulatory Impact Assessment estimates that between 122,000 to 171,000 employees in the private sector are discriminated against in this way with respect to pensions.

The Regulations make it unlawful for an employer to provide a benefit to a partner, but only a partner of the opposite sex. Thus, they apply and render unlawful the practice that led to the historic litigation in *Grant v South West Trains Ltd* [1998] IRLR 206, culminating in the European Court of Justice.

The Government's Regulatory Impact Assessment also identifies terms and conditions which may be available to heterosexual employees, but not to lesbians, gay men and bisexual employees. 'These may include time off for dependants, special leave or travel expenses paid.' In that connection, some employers currently give preference to parents in holiday allocation, or provide certain benefits only to employees with children – for example, nursery vouchers, loans for school fees, or even subsidised creches. Although lesbians and gay men do have children, they are less likely to, so that these could be challenged as being indirectly discriminatory, provided the benefits were not directly linked to marital status so as to fall within the exception discussed below. The benefits would then have to be justified by the employer despite their discriminatory impact as being a proportionate means of achieving a legitimate aim. It should not be difficult for an employer to establish its legitimate aim, but showing a proportionate means may be more difficult. The point could be made on behalf of the applicant that the employer could adopt a 'cafeteria'-style benefit system, under which all employees are entitled to benefits of a certain value and are free to choose those which are most appropriate for them.

Similarly, some employers give parents the first choice of holiday dates, on the basis that they need to fit their holidays around school vacations. This may be laudable, but it is likely to adversely impact gay employees who may have other reasons for needing time off in school holiday periods, such as that the employee's partner is a teacher.

Stonewall's *Guidelines for Employers* to the Regulations (2004) suggests that policies should state that the following are available to same-sex partners or nominees of the employee's choice:
- bereavement leave
- parental leave and adoptive parental leave
- relocation allowances
- carer's leave
- travel benefits

- discounts on the company's or other services
- private healthcare.

Exception for benefits dependent on marital status

Lesbian and gay couples are currently legally unable to marry, although this legal disability is likely to be removed when the Civil Partnerships Bill, promised in the Queen's Speech in November 2003, is enacted. The most common benefit provided to married couples, and thus prima facie indirectly discriminatory against gay and lesbian couples, is survivor's benefits under an occupational pension scheme. This has been a key issue for campaigners for lesbian and gay rights.

Most public sector schemes still only give benefits to married partners and it has been estimated that around a quarter of private sector pension schemes do not provide pensions to unmarried partners. However, the Government has chosen to exclude survivor's benefits and all other benefits determined by reference to marital status from coverage of the right not to be discriminated against on grounds of sexual orientation. The controversial exclusion is set out in reg 25, which provides:

> 'Nothing in Parts II or III shall render unlawful anything which prevents or restricts access to a benefit by reference to marital status.'

Thus, benefits which are aimed exclusively at married couples will continue to be permissible and will not constitute unlawful indirect discrimination on grounds of sexual orientation, notwithstanding the fact that it is not currently possible for same-sex partners to marry in the UK. As noted, in particular, the exclusion means that survivor benefits in an occupational pension scheme can continue to be made only available to the spouse of the deceased employee. It also excludes challenges to any other benefit that might be provided to spouses only, for example relocation allowances, or coverage under private health insurance.

The Government regards this exclusion as justified by recital 22 to the Framework Employment Directive. This says that: 'This Directive is without prejudice to national laws on marital status and the benefits dependent thereon.'

This is one of the two aspects of the new Regulations that is the subject of the judicial review challenge, *Amicus — MSF section v Secretary of State for Trade and Industry*.

In the explanatory memorandum for the Sexual Orientation Regulations, the Government has elaborated upon its reasoning: 'Regulation 25 reflects the fact that treatment by reference to marital status is outside the scope of the Directive. Article 3 of the Directive states that it applies 'only within the limits of the areas of competence conferred on the Community.' Distinctions between the rights of married and unmarried people are outside the scope of Community competence, because marriage is a family law concept that is regulated by the laws of the Member States.' Alternatively, in the judicial review proceedings the Government is putting forward the defence that the exclusion of benefits awarded by reference to marital status from the ambit of the Regulations is justified, 'having regard to the Government's policy to support marriage as an institution, the practical implications and likely adverse effects of including such benefits within the ambit of the Regulations, and the Government's plans to introduce legislation permitting the registration of civil partnerships for same sex couples.'

So far as the scope of the Directive is concerned, it clearly covers pay, and this includes benefits such as those payable to a partner on a pension holder's death. The Government's view that indirect discrimination against lesbian and gay couples is permissible because of recital 22 treats the preamble to the Directive, not as an aid to its interpretation but as if it was part of the language of the Directive itself. In any event, the applicability of the recital to survivors' benefits provided by occupational pension schemes is by no means clear-cut. One reading of the relevant sentence is that the 'benefits' referred to in the recital are not those dependent on 'marital status' generally (so as to encompass benefits linked to marital status under private occupational schemes) but rather those dependent on 'national laws on marital status'. On that reading, this would permit exceptions for social security schemes, such as widow's benefit, but would not extend to occupational schemes, since occupational schemes are governed by their own rules and not by national laws on marital status.

The contention that rights of married and unmarried people are outside the scope of Community competence was unconvincing from the start, given that Equal Treatment Directive 76/207 states in terms that 'the principle of equal treatment shall mean that there shall be no discrimination whatsoever on grounds of sex either directly or indirectly by reference in particular to marital or family status' and our own Sex Discrimination Act, implementing that Directive, expressly prohibits a distinction in favour of unmarried people compared with those who are married. The argument has been further undermined by the decision of the European Court of Justice in *KB v National Health Service Pensions Agency* [2004] IRLR 240. In this case, a female nurse used Article 141 of the EU Treaty to challenge the exclusion by the NHS pension scheme of her female-to-male transsexual partner from the right to a survivor's pension because they are not legally married. The European Court ruled that there was a violation of Article 141 in principle because UK law prohibiting transsexuals from marrying was held by the European Court of Human Rights in the *Goodwin* case to be in breach of the right to marry under the European Convention. This certainly suggests that the ECJ does not agree that access to benefits by reference to marital status is outside the scope of Directives in this area.

The first stage of the judicial review is likely to be resolved by the time this book is published, but it will also be important to monitor the terms of the Civil Partnership Bill when it is published. The Government is committed to providing that the legal rights and responsibilities of those who enter into civil partnerships will include equivalent treatment to married couples for a range of employment-related benefits. It is understood that the Sexual Orientation Regulations will be amended to provide for this, although it is highly unlikely that this will be retrospective.

Occupational pension schemes

The Employment Equality (Sexual Orientation) Regulations 2003 (Amendment) Regulations also came into force on 1 December. These introduced a new reg 9A, which provides that it is unlawful for the trustees and managers of occupational pension schemes to discriminate against a member or prospective member of the pension scheme in carrying out any of their functions relating to admission of members into the scheme or the treatment of members of it.

Other key sexual orientation discrimination issues

Emblems

Lesbians and gay men sometimes wish to wear jewellery, badges or other emblems showing their pride in their sexual orientation. Some readers may remember *Boychuk v H J Symons Holding Ltd* [1977] IRLR 395, an early unfair dismissal case in which it was held not to have been unfair to dismiss a woman employed as an audit clerk because she insisted upon wearing a white badge which said 'Lesbians Ignite' in large red letters. The EAT approved the principle that 'it is within an employer's discretion to instruct an employee not to wear some sign or symbol that could be offensive to fellow-employees and customers.'

Any badge with large red letters might still be considered problematic, but it is interesting to consider the analysis if the employer sought to ban rainbow pins, or Gay Pride, FF or MM earrings, for example. In order to determine whether there was less favourable treatment on grounds of sexual orientation, a comparison would have to be made with how the employer treats symbols of heterosexuality. If the employer prohibits a woman from wearing a lesbian symbol at work, it might be said that this can only be nondiscriminatory if it also

bans women at work from wearing an engagement ring.

Arrest records

Gross indecency is an offence involving consenting sex between men, which becomes unlawful if it took place in public, or if more than two people were present, or if one party was under the age of consent. By definition, the law only applies to gay and bisexual men. There is no heterosexual equivalent.

Because of the practice of 'cottaging', many gay and bisexual men have convictions for gross indecency and therefore criminal records. According to barrister and former Stonewall worker Anya Palmer, 'the vast majority of convictions involve sex which was unlawful because it took place in a park or other public place.'

The European Court of Human Rights has held that British law is a contravention of Convention rights and the offence is in the process of being repealed. However, past convictions for this offence presumably will continue to show up in criminal record checks.

Thus, where an employer operates a policy whereby anyone with a criminal conviction, or even an arrest record, is not considered for employment, this is likely to operate to the disadvantage of some gay and bisexual men. If challenged via an indirect discrimination claim, an employer would have to show that a blanket policy of exclusion was a proportionate means of achieving a legitimate aim. This is unlikely to be held to be the case, except where the particular job is such that such a policy can be regarded as appropriate, as in *X v Y* [2003] IRLR 561, where the applicant was dismissed from his job working with youth offenders after he had been cautioned for gross indecency with another man in a public toilet and failed to disclose the fact that he had committed a criminal offence to his employers.

If the employer took particular exception to the offence of 'gross indecency', in comparison with other criminal offences having less of an adverse impact on gay and bisexual men, this would also have to be shown to be objectively justifiable.

The ACAS Guide suggests that: 'Employers may wish to consider that the laws relating to gay men have changed significantly over time. It is possible that applicants may have acquired a criminal conviction many years before for a matter no longer unlawful (such as consensual adult gay sex). This is unlikely to have any bearing on the individual's skills and suitability for the job or training advertised. Generally a subsequent change in the criminal law does not affect whether an existing sentence becomes spent, the sentence still stands.'

Therefore, in view of the changes to the law, employers asking for details of criminal convictions on application forms might wish to state that convictions for gross indecency will not be taken into account.

Discrimination against those with HIV

Gay men are disproportionately affected by HIV. Discrimination against those with HIV, or AIDS, will be prima facie indirectly discriminatory, whether the individual's condition is symptomatic and classified as a disability under the Disability Discrimination Act 1995, or asymptomatic and currently unprotected under the DDA. Such indirect discrimination might arise where an employer had a practice of HIV testing, for example.

Where a gay man is stereotyped as likely to be HIV-positive that will amount to direct discrimination on grounds of sexual orientation, or harassment, in that the same stereotype would not be applied to a heterosexual man.

It is also likely to involve sex discrimination, in that the same stereotype would not be applied to a lesbian. This is an issue which arose many years ago when an airline attempted to recruit only female cabin staff on grounds that a large proportion of male applicants were gay and would pose a health risk if they were HIV-positive. The airline backed down on being threatened with sex discrimination action.

Enforcement

Complaints of discrimination or harassment on grounds of sexual orientation by employers and most other complaints of discrimination under the new Regulations will be heard by employment tribunals. The statutory provisions here are the same as for complaints under the Race Relations Act and Disability Discrimination Acts.

In most cases, an applicant who is claiming sexual orientation discrimination will have to assert their sexual orientation as part of their application. This may raise concerns amongst lesbian, gay and bisexual applicants who are not 'out' or not out fully that their orientation will become a matter of public record, and may be subject to publicity in the media, if they bring a complaint.

The Employment Tribunals Rules of Procedure allow for a restricted reporting order to protect the identity of the applicant in a case which involves allegations of sexual misconduct and for a register deletion order in a case which appears to involve allegations of the commission of a sexual offence. In *X v Stevens* [2003] IRLR 411, the EAT held that even where there is no allegation of sexual misconduct or a sexual offence, employment tribunals and the EAT have power to make orders analogous to a restricted reporting order and/or a register deletion order, or to make some provision in respect of confidentiality, so as to protect the identity of an applicant where there has been a finding of fact that they would be deterred from bringing proceedings under the Sex Discrimination Act in the absence of such an order. According to Burton J, this power is necessary in order to give effect to Article 6 of the Equal Treatment Directive, which obliges Member States to 'introduce into their national legal systems such measures as are necessary to enable all persons who consider themselves wronged by failure to apply to them the principle of equal treatment ... to pursue their claims by judicial process.' This, the EAT held, requires an interpretation of the respective rules so as to ensure that an applicant bringing a claim under the Sex Discrimination Act is not hampered or deterred by an inappropriately restrictive reading of the powers of either tribunal.

Commenting on that decision in the IRLR *Highlights* [2003] IRLR 383, I noted that the Framework Employment Directive contains comparable provisions to Article 6 of the Equal Treatment Directive, and therefore would appear to be covered by the EAT's ruling in this case. I suggested that requests for confidentiality might be particularly relevant in certain sexual orientation claims. This appears to be view of the DTI as well, which asserts that: 'If an individual wishes to bring a complaint of discrimination or harassment under the Sexual Orientation Regulations in an employment tribunal, but does not wish her sexual orientation to enter the public domain, she may ask the tribunal to make

a Register Deletion Order and/or a Restricted Reporting Order, which would allow her to remain anonymous in the proceedings.'

There is a potential conflict here between the right to privacy and the right not be deterred from having a fair hearing on the one hand, and the principles of freedom of the press and open justice on the other. Whether all lesbians and gay men who are not 'out' will be regarded as having a right to have their discrimination complaint heard without reporting in the media is one of the many issues of principle that will have to be resolved under the Regulations.

Disability discrimination

The Disability Discrimination Act 1995 (Amendment) Regulations 2003 implement the disability strand of the EU Framework Employment Directive. The changes to the DDA will take effect from 1 October 2004.

Many of the changes of practical significance are those which affect all the different strands of discrimination covered by the new Regulations, including a freestanding definition of harassment, provision for unlawful acts after a relationship has ended and changes to the burden of proof. These were discussed in the first part of this book.

However, the Directive contains special provisions concerning disability, which have proved to be both complex, and difficult to implement within the established framework of the DDA.

New definitions of discrimination

Probably the most important change to the DDA is the addition of a new definition of unlawful discrimination covering direct discrimination 'on the ground of' a disabled person's disability. This will sit alongside the existing two definitions of discrimination in the DDA – less favourable treatment for a reason relating to disability and failure to make a reasonable adjustment.

The Framework Directive specifies that 'there shall be no direct or indirect discrimination whatsoever' on any of the relevant grounds covered, including the 'ground' of disability. Direct discrimination is defined as occurring 'where one person is treated less favourably than other is, has been or would be treated in a comparable situation', for this purpose, on the ground of disability. The same definition is used for discrimination on grounds of religion or belief, or sexual orientation. It is also essentially the same definition as currently found in the Sex Discrimination and Race Relations Acts.

DDA 1995, s 5(1) as currently in force, specifies that:

'an employer discriminates against a disabled person if –
(a) for a reason which relates to the disabled person's disability, he treats him less favourably than he treats or would treat others to whom that reason does not or would not apply; and
(b) he cannot show that the treatment in question is justified.'

This is a broader definition than that in the Directive because it covers discrimination which is not just on the 'ground' of disability as such, but also discrimination which 'relates' to the person's disability. However, as limb (b) makes clear, this discrimination can be 'justified' by the employer, whereas the Directive makes no provision for discrimination on the 'ground' of disability to be justified, except where genuine occupational requirements apply. There is, of course, a well-developed body of case law on the principles for determining when disability discrimination is justified, most notably the Court of Appeal's decision in *Jones v Post Office* [2001] EWCA Civ 558, [2001] IRLR 384, CA.

The way the Government decided to reconcile these two definitions was to include them both in the revised DDA. Section 5(1) will remain exactly the same and will become s 3A(1). As is the case with the existing definition, new s 3A(3) provides that treatment is justified for the purposes of s 3A(1)(b):

'if, but only if, the reason for it is both material to the circumstances of the particular case and substantial.'

However, new s 3A(4) states:

'But treatment of a disabled person cannot be justified under subsection (3) if it amounts to direct discrimination falling within subsection (5).'

Direct discrimination is then defined in s 3A(5) as follows:

'A person directly discriminates against a disabled person if, on the ground of the disabled person's disability, he treats the disabled person less favourably than he treats or would treat a person not having that particular disability whose relevant circumstances, including his abilities, are the same as, or not materially different from, those of the disabled person.'

Direct discrimination and disability-related discrimination

What is the distinction between these two definitions and when will each apply? The answer, unfortunately, is by no means clear.

Referring to the new definition, the explanatory memorandum issued by the Department for Work and Pensions when the Regulations were laid before Parliament says: 'The intention of the changes is to outlaw, for example, prejudicial treatment imposed simply because a person is disabled, such as a "blanket ban" on the employment of persons with a disability. Justification of such treatment has always been unlikely, but the subsections now make this explicit.'

This, in itself, would be a very narrow definition, little more than a 'for the avoidance of doubt' clause. Treatment on the ground of disability is obviously also for a reason related to disability. As the DWP acknowledges, it is highly improbable that a 'blanket ban' or other displays of prejudice would be regarded as a 'material and substantial reason' for less favourable treatment so as to fall within the definition of justification.

By contrast, the Disability Rights Commission, in its draft Code of Practice on employment and occupation issued in September 2003, understandably emphasised the potential breadth of the new definition, even going so far as to label the existing definition 'residual less favourable treatment' and asserting that 'direct discrimination is the more important of the two' definitions. Underlying this is that 'direct discrimination', as newly defined, is incapable of justification by an employer, thereby circumventing the restrictions imposed by the Court of Appeal case law on justification.

Only the tribunals and the courts will be able to decide the precise scope of the new definition and the distinction between new direct discrimination and what is likely to be called (and what we will call here) 'disability-related' discrimination. What seems likely is that the new definition will cover considerably more than mere prejudice, even though there will be difficult issues to determine as to when an employer's act is on grounds of disability as opposed to being for a disability-related reason.

Direct discrimination certainly covers the employer who does not wish to employ anyone who is disabled. This is increasingly rare, though some small firms, brought within the scope of the DDA for the first time, may be caught out.

Much more importantly, the new definition of direct discrimination will cover the employer who has prejudices about particular kinds of disabilities, or, even more realistically, about employing people with particular kinds of disabilities for particular kinds of work. For example, an employer who would not employ a person with a history of mental illness for certain jobs. If the employer rejects the application by someone with a history of mental illness out of hand, without investigating the individual circumstances and how they relate to the particular needs of the job, that is likely to be categorised as discrimination on grounds of the disability, rather than for a reason related to it.

The concept of direct discrimination also is likely to cover stereotyping, probably the most common form of discrimination against disabled people. If an employer treats a disabled person less favourably than it treats other people because of the employer's stereotypical, generalised assumptions about the disability or its effects, the treatment is likely to be regarded as being on the ground of the disability. This is because an employer would not normally make generalised assumptions about a non-disabled person's ability to do the job, but would instead consider his or her individual abilities. The DRC draft Code gives a useful example: 'A blind woman is not short-listed for a job involving computers because the employer wrongly assumes that blind people cannot use them. The employer makes no attempt to look at the individual circumstances. This would amount to direct discrimination and would be unlawful.'

Direct discrimination will also encompass cases where the employer claims to be acting for a disability-neutral or a disability-related reason and, upon investigation, this turns out to be a pretext for a decision made on the basis of a stereotype.

It is important to bear in mind, in this context, that it will not be necessary for a tribunal to find that disability was the sole, or even the main, reason for the less favourable treatment in order for it to be found to be 'on the ground' of disability. Case law under the Sex Discrimination Act, such as *O'Neill v Governors of St Thomas More School* [1996] IRLR 372, EAT establishes that what must be applied is an objective test of causal connection. The event or factor alleged to be causative of the matter complained of need not be the only or even the main cause of the result complained of. It is enough if it is an effective cause. This principle was applied in a disability discrimination context by the EAT (Judge J McMullen QC presiding) in *Summer Bridge Doors Ltd v Pickering* (21 March 2003).

There is clearly a conceptual distinction between discrimination on the ground of a person's disability as such, and discrimination for a disability-related reason. However, it is hard at this stage to see a bright line between the two. For a start, there is an issue as to how the wording on the 'ground' of disability will be interpreted by the tribunals and courts. If it is viewed in comparison with 'for a reason related to' disability, it could be interpreted quite narrowly. As noted, direct discrimination on the ground of disability is automatically unlawful whatever its justification and our tribunals tend not to like to have their opportunity to assess justice taken out of their hands. On the other hand, the Sex Discrimination Act prohibits discrimination on 'grounds' of sex and that has been interpreted very widely, so as to encompass discrimination on grounds of pregnancy.

The difficulties posed by the statutory language might be said to be illustrated by one of the examples of direct discrimination given in the DRC's draft Code: 'A disabled person with serious long-term back pain takes six months' sick leave because of his disability, and is dismissed by his employer. A non-disabled fellow employee also takes six months' sick leave (because he has broken his leg) but is not dismissed. The difference in treatment is attributable to the employer's unwillingness to employ disabled staff. This is unlawful direct discrimination. The comparator is a person not having the disability in question but who has also taken six months' sick leave.'

Leave to one side that the scenario is rather far-fetched in that if the employer was unwilling to employ disabled staff, it is unlikely to have recruited the disabled person. The real problem is that the relevant circumstances in the two situations arguably are not the same in that the employer would expect the person with a broken leg to make a full recovery, whereas the disabled person has a 'serious long-term condition'. If the case went to a tribunal, the employer would say that it was not 'unwilling' to employ disabled people, and that its decision was based on the amount of absence and the prospects for recovery. In other words, the employer would acknowledge that the dismissal was for a disability-related reason and attempt to argue that it was justified.

Take another of the examples in the draft Code: 'A disabled woman who uses a wheelchair applies for a job. She can do the job but the employer wrongly assumes that the wheelchair will cause an obstruction in the office. He therefore gives the job to a person who is no more suitable for the job but who is not a wheelchair-user. The employer has therefore treated the woman less favourably than the other person by not giving her the job. The treatment was on the ground of the woman's disability.'

At first sight, this certainly looks to fall within the category of direct discrimination. But if the case went to a tribunal, the employer will mount an argument that the reason the woman was rejected was because of his concerns about safety, and that he would treat any applicant who raised potential safety concerns similarly. Therefore, he will say that this treatment was not on grounds of the particular disability (assuming that wheelchair use is a disability in any event, rather than a consequence of an impairment), but on grounds of health and safety, albeit that it is for a reason related to the disability.

Employers will always be advised to couch their reasons for a decision that is being challenged as discriminatory in neutral or disability-related terms so as to leave open the possibility for justification. The principles that will be developed by the courts for determining on which side of the line particular cases go will be a key issue over the next few years.

Burden of proof

The new provisions relating to the burden of proof (see Chapter 1) will apply to DDA cases from 1 October 2004.

The impact of the new burden of proof is rather less clear in the case of disability discrimination than in other areas of discrimination law. In any case of alleged disability discrimination, it is for the applicant to show that they are a disabled person within the meaning of the Act. This burden would appear to be unchanged by the new provisions.

Conversely, in a case of disability-related discrimination, it is clear law that the burden shifts to the employer to justify the less favourable treatment of the applicant for a reason that relates to their disability than the treatment of others to whom the reason does not apply.

Where the new burden of proof may make a difference is as regards establishing the reason for the treatment and whether it is on the grounds of disability or, alternatively, for a reason related to disability. Here, if the disabled applicant is able to establish that they have been treated less favourably than a comparator whose circumstances were not materially different, it is arguable that the burden should shift to the employer to show what the reason for the less favourable treatment was and that it was not the disabled person's disability. In such a case, it might be said, at least on the basis of the *Anya* decision, that this finding without any contradictory evidence would be sufficient to justify a finding of discrimination. It would also be for the employer to show, if it was so contended, that the reason for the treatment did not relate to the disabled person's disability either or, alternatively, if it did, that the treatment was justified. For a definitive answer as to how the new burden of proof provisions work in a DDA context, we must await decisions of the appellate courts.

Changes to the duty to adjust

The duty on employers under the DDA 1995, s 6 to make reasonable adjustments in relation to disabled people is broadly the same, but the Regulations do make a number of significant changes.

The scope of the duty is widened from the existing duty to make adjustments as regards 'arrangements made by or on behalf of an employer' to cover any 'provision, criterion or practice applied by or on behalf of an employer', which places 'the disabled person concerned at a substantial disadvantage in comparison with persons who are not disabled.' The definitions section of the Regulations defines 'provision, criterion or practice' as including 'any arrangements'. Moreover, whereas s 6(2) currently limits the duty of reasonable adjustment so that it does not appear to apply to cases of discrimination by dismissal or by subjecting an employee to a detriment, this limitation is removed and the adjustment duty will apply at any stage of the employment process: from arrangements for selection through to dismissal.

This is explained in the explanatory memorandum as follows: 'where it is reasonable to do so, an employer will be required to modify the application of any provision, criterion or practice which causes more than a minor or trivial disadvantage to a

particular disabled employee to the extent needed to remove the disadvantage.' The following example is given: 'where an employer requires all employees to work from 9 am to 5 pm, it might be reasonable to adjust that rule in the case of a particular disabled employee so that he/she can work flexible hours in order to accommodate additional breaks to overcome fatigue arising from the disability.'

The draft Code of Practice adds:

'"Provisions, criteria and practices" encompass matters such as arrangements for determining to whom employment should be offered, and terms, conditions or arrangements on which employment, promotion, a transfer, training or any other benefit is offered or afforded. The duty to make reasonable adjustments therefore applies, for example, to selection and interview procedures and the arrangements for using premises for such procedures as well as to job offers, contractual arrangements and working conditions.'

An interesting example is given for this: 'It is normal practice for a call centre to employ supervisors on a full-time basis. A woman with sickle cell anaemia applies for a job as a supervisor. Because of pain and fatigue relating to her condition she asks to be able to do the job on a part-time basis. The employer agrees that the post could be offered on this basis. The hours of work which are offered amount to an adjustment to a working practice. This is likely to be a reasonable adjustment.'

This illustrates just how wide the duty to make adjustments under the DDA in respect of a disability can be, as compared with rights under other legislation to request part-time working.

Section 6 of the DDA sets out a number of factors which, in particular, should be taken into account in determining whether it is reasonable for an adjustment to have to be made by an employer. Two new factors are added by the Regulations:
* 'the nature of his activities and the size of his undertaking' and
* 'where the step would be taken in relation to a private household, the extent to which taking it would –

(i) disrupt that household, or

(ii) disrupt any person residing there.'

The explanatory memorandum says about the latter: 'Even if the financial cost would be minimal, an adjustment may not be reasonable if it would entail disruption to the household (eg repeated re-arrangement of furniture) or disturbance to persons who live there (eg by requiring them to change their routines in order to accommodate the disabled person).'

The Act also sets out some specific examples of adjustments that an employer might have to take, which were illustrated by examples in the 1996 Code. The specific examples are changed only to a minor extent by the Regulations: 'altering his working hours' becomes 'altering his hours of working or training', 'assigning him to a different place of work' becomes 'assigning him to a different place of work or training', 'giving him, or arranging for him to be given, training' becomes 'giving, or arranging for, training or mentoring (whether for the disabled person or any other person)', and 'providing supervision' becomes 'providing supervision or other support'.

The draft Code points out that it might be reasonable for employers to have to take other steps, which are not given as examples in the Act. According to the DRC, these steps could include:
- permitting flexible working
- participating in supported employment schemes, such as Workstep
- employing a support worker to assist a disabled employee
- modifying disciplinary or grievance procedures
- adjusting redundancy selection criteria, and
- modifying performance-related pay arrangements.

Justifying failure to make reasonable adjustment

The Regulations remove the possibility of an employer justifying a failure to make an adjustment that it is reasonable for a person to have to make.

This is a part of the DDA that has been interpreted inconsistently by the tribunals and appellate courts. Some cases have held that if an adjustment is found to be 'reasonable' for an employer to have to make, it is illogical to go on to find that the employer was justified in being unreasonable by not making it. Other decisions have taken the view that the current wording of the DDA 1995 clearly provides such a defence for an employer and that, moreover, that defence must be assessed in accordance with the comparatively low threshold of justification on the employer established by the Court of Appeal in *Jones v Post Office*.

The Court of Appeal is reviewing this case law in several cases before it in the first part of 2004, but the concept of justifying a failure to make a reasonable adjustment is regarded by the Government as not compatible with the Framework Directive, which requires an adjustment to be made if it is reasonable so to do. Accordingly, the justification defence is removed with effect from 1 October 2004.

Scope

The Framework Directive does not allow exclusions from its scope, except where these are specified in the Directive. The only relevant exclusion set out in the Directive for DDA purposes is that Member States may provide that the Directive 'shall not apply to the armed forces' as regards disability (and age).

Accordingly, as of 1 October 2004, the small employer exclusion in the DDA of employees of firms with fewer than 15 employees will be removed, so that the Act will cover all employment and all employers, whatever their size.

The DDA has a number of specific exclusions, including police officers, prison officers and firefighters. These are brought within the scope of the legislation on 1 October 2004, as are employees on ships, planes and hovercrafts registered in the UK. Practical work experience is also covered for the first time, to the extent that the trainee concerned is not an employee of the person providing them with the practical work experience.

In addition, in common with the other strands of the Framework Directive, rights will also be extended to office holders, partners in firms, barristers and advocates (and pupils in their chambers). These aspects are discussed below.

Office holders

The difference between the disability strand and the other strands is that the extension of scope to office holders under the DDA incorporates not only a duty not to discriminate on the prohibited ground, but also a duty of reasonable adjustment. To take the example of chairmen and members of employment tribunals, or of the EAT, this will mean that there is a duty to make adjustments to any provision, criterion or practice applied by or on behalf of the employer or any physical feature of premises that places a disabled person at a substantial disadvantage with people who are not disabled. In some circumstances, this might entail changes to sitting times or the way in which hearings are conducted, for example, such as to incorporate extra breaks.

Identifying the person who has the duty of reasonable adjustment (or not to discriminate) in the case of office holders, however, is by no means straightforward. It is dealt with in detail in reg 4F. This is because the person who makes the appointment to the office is not necessarily the same person as is responsible for their working conditions once they are holding the office. The Regulations prohibit discrimination by, and impose duties to make adjustments on, 'relevant persons'. This is then defined as, in a case relating to an appointment to an office or post, the person with the power to make that appointment; and in a case relating to a working condition, the person with power to determine that working condition (or, where there is no such person, the person with the power to make the appointment). Thus, in the case of the appointment of members of the Disability Rights Commission, the relevant person would be the Secretary of State for Work and Pensions. However, the relevant person

responsible for making adjustments to the working conditions or office environment so that DRC members can carry out their work, would be the Commission itself.

Partnerships

The Regulations confer on a partner or applicant for partnership similar rights against the firm as enjoyed by applicants for employment or employees.

Section 6B makes clear that the duty to make reasonable adjustments as regards partners or prospective partners falls on the firm. Section 6B(4) provides for the costs of reasonable adjustments for a disabled person to be a charge on the firm. It stipulates that the extent to which such costs should be borne by the disabled person who is or becomes a partner in the firm 'shall not exceed such amount as is reasonable, having regard in particular to the proportion in which he is entitled to share in the firm's profits.'

Contract workers

The DDA makes it unlawful for a principal to discriminate against a contract worker, and requires the principal to make reasonable adjustments in respect of a contract worker, unless the worker's employer (eg an employment agency) is required to make the adjustment.

There have been some modifications to the existing statutory provisions in this respect, and the DDA 1995, s 12 and reg 7 of the Disability Discrimination (Employment) Regulations 1996 are replaced by new s 4B. This sets out the rule that it is unlawful for a person providing work for a disabled person who is a contract worker to discriminate against him, and also that harassment by a person providing contract work is unlawful.

New sub-ss 4B(4) and 4B(5) require an employer of a disabled contract worker to make reasonable adjustments where 'all or most of the principals to whom he is or might be supplied' apply a provision, criterion or practice, or where a physical feature of the premises they occupy, are likely 'on each occasion' to put the disabled contract worker at a substantial disadvantage in comparison with persons who are not disabled. The DWP explanatory memorandum gives the following example: 'where an employer supplies a word processor operator who is blind to work for several principals, the employer might have to provide her with a specially adapted portable computer because she would otherwise be at a similar substantial disadvantage in doing the work wherever she does it. Each of the principals would have to cooperate by letting her use the computer, provided it was compatible with their systems.'

Barristers and advocates

In common with the other grounds for discrimination covered by the new Regulations, barristers are brought within the scope of the DDA. Previously, neither barristers nor pupils in chambers had rights under the DDA's employment provisions because they are not persons in 'employment' within the meaning of the statutory definition.

The new provisions not only make it unlawful to discriminate against a barrister because he has a disability, they also provide for barristers and barristers' clerks to be under a duty to make reasonable adjustments for disabled prospective pupils, pupils, prospective tenants and tenants. Section 7B(2) extends the duty to cases where barristers practice from sets of chambers. It makes clear that in such a case the duty to make reasonable adjustments is 'a duty on each of them to take such steps as it is reasonable, in all the circumstances of the case, for him to have to take'.

Parallel provisions apply in the case of advocates and their clerks in Scotland, adapted to take account of the fact that Scottish advocates do not practice in sets of chambers.

Qualifications bodies

Qualifications bodies are also brought within the scope of the DDA for the first time. It will be unlawful for a body which confers professional or trade qualifications to discriminate against a disabled person in the arrangements made for the purpose of determining upon whom to confer a professional or trade qualification, by refusing to confer, or in the terms on which it confers, such a qualification or by withdrawing or varying the terms of a qualification.

'Qualifications body' is defined as 'any authority or body which can confer a professional or trade qualification'. However, this does not extend to an institution of further and higher education, or discrimination by a school against its pupils.

'Professional or trade qualification' is defined widely as including 'any authorisation or qualification that is needed for, or facilitates engagement in, a particular profession or trade.' 'Trade' is separately defined by the DDA as including any business.

This wide definition would appear to encompass general academic and vocational qualifications, including GCSEs and A Levels on the one hand, or a driving licence on the other, as well as specific qualifications. Attaining such qualifications would appear to be covered since attaining them 'facilitates engagement in' a number of professions or jobs.

There are special provisions concerning 'competence standards' – an academic, medical or other standard used to determine whether a person has a particular level of competence or ability. Section 14A(3), which covers a claim that the application by a qualifications body of a competence standard to a disabled person constitutes unlawful discrimination for a reason related to disability, is a unique example of the DDA using the 'proportionate means of achieving a legitimate aim' test of justification found in the indirect discrimination provisions of the other Regulations rather than the reasonable adjustments approach normally used in the employment sections of the DDA to deal with potential cases of indirect discrimination. According to the DWP, 'this is because it is considered highly desirable, and in the public interest, that qualifications bodies should be able to apply one professional standard, applying equally to all applicants, rather than being obliged to adjust that standard on a case-by-case basis. The "knowledge" test for London taxi drivers is a good example of such a standard.'

'It follows that a qualifications body will be obliged to justify a competence standard which particularly disadvantages persons having a particular disability by reference to the test of objective justification. It will, therefore, have to show that the standard is justified by reference to a legitimate aim and is a proportionate way of achieving that aim. This is likely to entail the provision of clear evidence that any standard is genuinely necessary and fundamental to the requirements of the trade or profession in order to ensure competence in that trade.'

'By contrast, in cases not involving the application of a "competence standard" (for example, cases relating to the practical way in which qualifications bodies assess standards, such as the conditions under which candidates have to sit examinations leading up to a professional qualification), the duty to make reasonable adjustments will apply (see s 14B, below). In such cases, the ordinary defence of justification set out in s 3A(2), rather than the defence of objective justification applying to competence standards set out in s 14A(3), will apply.'

Section 14B places a duty of adjustment on qualifications bodies, where a provision, criterion or practice, other than a competence standard, or a physical feature of premises occupied by the qualifications body, places the disabled person at a substantial disadvantage. According to the DWP explanatory memorandum, 'this could include allowing extra time, supplying the exam papers in alternative accessible format or supplying a separate, accessible room for a disabled candidate.'

Discriminatory advertisements

At present, it is not unlawful to publish an advertisement indicating an intention to discriminate on grounds of disability. Use of a discriminatory advertisement by an employer obliges a tribunal to assume, unless the contrary is proved, that the reason for a disabled applicant being refused a job was related to their disability.

The Regulations replace this provision with a specific prohibition on discriminatory advertisements. This makes it unlawful for a person intending to confer a relevant appointment or benefit to publish a discriminatory advertisement or cause such an advertisement to be published. The advertisement will be unlawful where it:

'indicates, or might reasonably be understood to indicate, that an application will or may be determined to any extent by reference to –
(i) the applicant not having any disability, or any particular disability, or
(ii) any reluctance of the person determining the application to comply with a duty to make reasonable adjustments … '.

Thus, as the explanatory memorandum points out, 'it could be unlawful to say in an advertisement that only persons in perfect health need apply.'

However, the Regulations go on to provide that an advertisement will not be unlawful where it would in fact be lawful to determine the application in the way indicated in the advertisement. According to the explanatory memorandum, 'for example, it would not be unlawful to say that persons applying for the position of train drivers must have a specific level of eyesight necessary for the performance of the essential functions of that post.'

Proceedings in respect of a contravention of the discriminatory advertisement provisions can only be brought by the Disability Rights Commission in the employment tribunal. If the tribunal upholds the complaint and it appears to the DRC that, unless restrained, the person concerned is likely to do a further unlawful act, then the Commission can apply to a county court for an injunction (or to a sheriff court in Scotland for an interdict). There is a similar enforcement procedure set out in the Regulations as regards instructions to discriminate and pressure to discriminate.

However, as it currently stands, the DDA applies to employers and others who publish or cause to be published a discriminatory advertisement. It does not prohibit newspapers and other third parties from publishing discriminatory advertisements on behalf of the person placing the advertisement. That gap is filled by provisions in the Government's draft Disability Bill, which was published late in 2003 and referred for consideration to a Parliamentary Joint Committee. This would extend the scope of the prohibition on discriminatory advertisements to cover third party publishers who publish a discriminatory advertisement.

Index

[all references are to page number]

KM 208